Raindrops on Roman – Overcoming Autism: A Message of Hope is a heartwarming and inspirational example of how early intervention, marshalling needed resources, and loving parental support can overcome autism. Elizabeth Scott exemplifies selfless commitment to her autistic son Roman and shares the invaluable day-to-day treatment strategies that ultimately resulted in his full recovery. Her story stresses the need for early diagnosis and a team approach to meet individual needs; the importance of parental acceptance, determination, and faith; as well as the rewards of skills and drills in a structured, warm, and loving family environment. Most importantly, her example of enabling Roman's recovery is a testament to this approach and offers hope and promise to parents of children with autism worldwide.

~ Kenneth C. Anderson, MD
Kraft Family Professor of Medicine,
Harvard Medical School
Chief, Division of Hematologic Neoplasia,
Dana-Farber Cancer Institute
Boston, MA

Elizabeth Scott has written a heart-warming story about a mother's love, faith, and dedication to her child. Her "Skills and Drills" program can be helpful to the growth and development of every child. An inspirational and informative book.

~ Doug Flutie
President of the Doug Flutie Jr.
Foundation For Autism
ABC/ESPN Television Sports Analyst

This book is a must read for all audiences. Her inspirational journey illustrates tangible teaching points for both families and health care professionals struggling to recognize the "red flags" of autism. Readers will be motivated to utilize the excellent resources provided in the book.

~ **Rebecca R. Hampton, MD**
Clinical Assistant Professor
Department of Pediatrics
Nationwide Children's Hospital/
The Ohio State University College of Medicine

Miraculous! Seeing is believing! Having personally seen Roman's transformation, autism recovery is not just possible; it is probable. Here enclosed are the "skills and drills" which have proven successful in Roman's amazing recovery... Elizabeth Scott sends a message of inspiration, hope, and love to parents of children with autism and normal children alike.

~ **Charles E. Toulson M.D.**
CEO, The Arthritis Institute
Plano, Texas

A beautifully written account of the journey from the devastating diagnosis of autism to the hard fought recovery of beautiful Roman. Elizabeth Scott exhibits extraordinary wisdom, knowledge, patience, and skills through her relentless and unwavering dedication to finding recovery to Roman's autism. A very candid, poignant story, and a must-read for parents facing the prospect of having to pull their child out of the clutches of autism. There is hope.

~ **Robert Beavers, Jr.**
Chairman/CEO Beavers Holdings
Retired Senior Vice President/
Director McDonalds Corporation

This is an incredible and encouraging story. You certainly taught me many lessons through your trials and tribulations. Your desire, determination and will to help Roman be the person he could be is such an inspiration to others. What an accomplishment for you all; most especially Roman.

~ **Paul Foster**
Reebok International Ltd

This book will inspire and motivate families to the possibilities for their child to overcome autism. Elizabeth writes about Roman's journey to recovery from autism with a mother's love, patience, dedication, and motivation to do what ever it takes to help her child. She describes her struggles and the daily demands that a child with autism has on a family and how she was able to cope and work with Roman. She includes important information presented in easy-to-understand language describing red flags to observe for autism, how and where to obtain diagnostic and therapeutic testing, and agencies to contact for needed services that are available at little or no cost. The Skills and Drills Lessons will provide useful instruction and suggestions for activities and creative play that parents can do to enhance their child's development. I know this book will be helpful to any family of a child with autism.

As an Occupational Therapist working with children and their families for thirty years I highly recommend Raindrops on Roman as a "must-have book" for Early Intervention and Children's Centers' lending libraries to share with their families of children with autism.

I am so proud of Elizabeth for writing her story and sharing her knowledge and experiences to help other families of children with autism. Thank you so much.

~ **Lynne Gillis**
OTR/L

Raindrops on Roman is an inspiring story of faith, family, hope and love. Elizabeth Scott delivers her message with skill and care — a terrific read for all parents!

~ **Dan Shaughnessy**
Boston Globe

This is truly a love story. It is imperative that this incredible account gets into the hands of every professional in the field of autism as well as the parents of all children who have received this devastating diagnosis

~ **Kate Rakini**
Editor

Raindrops on Roman

Overcoming Autism: A Message of Hope

A Mother Helps Her Son Recover from Autism!

Elizabeth Scott

Robert D. Reed Publishers • Bandon, OR

Robert D. Reed Publishers
P.O. Box 1992
Bandon, OR 97411
Phone: 541-347-9882; Fax: -9883
E-mail: 4bobreed@msn.com
Website: www.rdrpublishers.com

Editor: Kate Rakini
Cover Designer: Cleone L. Reed
Typesetter: Amy Cole

ISBN: 978-1-934759-24-0

Library of Congress Number: 2008941737

*Manufactured, Typeset, and Printed in the
United States of America*

Dedication

I dedicate this book
to my son, Roman, and husband, Tom:

Roman:

*I asked the impossible of you
and received the blessing.
You did everything I asked you to do and,
against all odds, you prevailed.
You did not give up
even when you wanted to,
and I will always love you.*

Tom:

*What a peaceful, gentle man;
a father any child would be proud of.
You helped us navigate a sinking ship,
stood by our side through all the despair,
and never let your faith waver.
Thank you for supporting and assisting
in the healing of our son,
and for being the husband and father
that we love, admire, and respect.
You have given me a life
filled with love and happiness.*

I Will Always Love You

Sweet child, I will always love you;
I will never leave you nor forsake you.
What joy you give me;
what courage you show me.
I respect your determination and fight to get better.
Though my heart breaks for your struggle
and what we go through,
your condition and limitations
only augment my love for you.
For I love you enough to stand the things I must do.
No matter what you need from me,
I will be there for you.
Anything that you can give,
that's all I'll ask of you.
Your love and strength inspire me;
I will be there for you.

Acknowledgments

My deepest thanks to:

First of all, my Lord and Savior, Jesus Christ, for answered prayer.

My mother, JoAnn Burton, for her endless support and encouragement, and for helping me maintain my faith and dedication. Through my mother I am able to see the love that only a mother can have for a child, which is all heart-felt and solely unconditional.

My father, Ron Burton Sr., who passed away before he could see his grandson recover, but who always believed he would be healed.

My four brothers, Steven, Ron Jr., Philip, and Paul, who have always been a tremendous support system. What a blessing to have four best friends throughout my entire life.

Special thanks to Life School's teachers and advocates who have made a profound difference in Roman's life.

Roman's principal, Mr. Joseph Mena, for his tremendous dedication to this outstanding school that demands a commitment to character, academic excellence, and leadership skills, and allows all students the opportunity to be the best they can be.

Roman's first grade teacher, Brandi Pietrzak, his kindergarten teacher, Leigh Ann Adames, and Assistant Principal Mindy Baeir, who always have high expectations for his behavior and performance, believe in him, encourage him daily, and always make him feel so proud.

The professionals who provided their knowledge and expertise to my book: Rachel Foster, Occupational Therapist; Lynn Gillis, Occupational Therapist; and Pam McCloskey, Occupational Therapist.

The Early Childhood Intervention speech and occupational therapists that taught me the techniques to use to bring Roman out of the world of autism: Melanie Hodges, ECI Coordinator; Carrie Delluge, Speech and Language Pathologist; and Jeanette Krajea, Occupational Therapist.

The preschool teachers who made Roman's first school experience a complete success: Andrea Hernandez, Paige Garza,

Dee Edwards, April Howard, and Tracey Rose.

The teachers and specialists at (LIPS) Language/Speech Intervention for Preschool Students: Laurie Strueby, Speech and Language Pathologist; Mary Rodriguez, Occupational Therapist; Susan Sprinkle, Licensed Specialist in School Psychology; and Stephanie Jean-Leeman, Teacher's Assistant.

Randy and Melanie McLeggan, thank you for your Godly insight and inspiration. We are so blessed to have your family as our extended family.

Jan Tharp, a lifelong family friend who has helped us in all of our endeavors, and especially my book.

Kimberly Armstrong, another parent who has been blessed with a "special" child. Thank you for your wisdom and guidance through the years.

My dear friends who have always supported my family: Regina Goodwin, Mollie Wagner, Gayle Beford, JoAnn Byron, Sally Salovitz, Karen Herring, and Deana Herd.

My publisher, Robert D. Reed, who believed in this topic and believed in me. He said, "Even if it helps just one person, then it's worth it." But we both know that many children do have a chance to overcome autism.

To Cleone Reed: The aesthetics of the cover are so captivating. Thank you for capturing and creating the vision I had for the book. It is said, "A picture say's a thousand words," and this picture say's it all.

To Amy Cole: The production of a book includes more than just the author, illustrator, and editor; there are so many unsung heros. Thank you for being one of mine. You provide the all important finishing touches of a book as interior designer/typesetter. I am so fortunate to have your loving touch.

My agent, Carol Schild, who helped me because she knew this story needed to be told. Thank you for finding a "home" for my book.

My editor, Kate Rakini, for all of your insight and passionate interest in this story.

Foreword

Elizabeth and I have known each other literally as long as we can remember. We grew up in suburban Boston; the Silver's at house number 10 and the Burton's at number 108. It's been that way since the early sixties and still that way today with my parents and Elizabeth's mother still in the same houses. However, with me now living in North Carolina and Elizabeth in Texas, we don't see each other nearly as often. I last saw Roman at his grandfather Ron's funeral when he had just turned two and Elizabeth was just beginning with his therapy. I remember he didn't speak and he did not want to be touched. It was quite obvious he was not a "typical" child. Although I did not see Roman or Elizabeth, I knew, from talking with my parents or Elizabeth's mom, about his autism and what Elizabeth was doing to try and overcome it. It was not until I read her story, however, that I realized what she, her husband, Tom, and Roman actually went through. It is truly remarkable what they did to save their son from a life of autism and lead him down a path where he will be able to enjoy life as independent adult, years from now.

With that in mind, I thought, what could I possibly write to preface their story? I know Elizabeth asked me to write something for her book because of my profession. I am a neonatologist and have cared for hundreds of premature babies in my career. Sadly, some of the sickest and smallest of the babies I care for survive the NICU only to live with sometimes lifelong disabilities, among them autism. But while I read her story I didn't think of the things I know from years of medical practice and as a father raising my own children, but I thought of two other things.

First and foremost, this is a story about a mother's love. There is no other way to explain what she endured to help Roman recover except love, pure and simple. My dear friend and mentor, Elizabeth's father Ron, always told us love others more than you love yourself, and the rest of life will be easy. Little did he know how that simple lesson would eventually translate into the incredible recovery of his own grandson. Everything Elizabeth did in her life unknowingly prepared her for taking care of Roman. She was a second mother to her two youngest brothers (and still is). In our days together in high school, she was a friend and helper to anyone who asked. She became an educator and spent her career prior to Roman as a teacher. She met and married Tom whose calm strength and support would allow her to do what she needed for their son. All of these things prepared her to do what she did for Roman, but without the fierce uncompromising love of a mother it would have never been accomplished.

The second thing that struck me was how much I learned from reading the book. Most of what is seen in the media about autism focuses on the cause(s). There is very little about a cure or recovery. I do not, by any means wish to discount the importance of finding the cause(s) of autism, but it is truly refreshing to read something offering hope to families who suffer with a child with autism. While this book does not offer recovery for every child with autism (some children are either too old or too severely affected), it does offer hope and possibility of recovery to many if they receive early and appropriate intervention. Hopefully, the new recommendations by the American Academy of Pediatrics (screening for autism for all children at 18 and 24 months), along with stories like Roman's will help countless children overcome autism in the future. And even for parents of children without autism, there is much to be learned from this book. The skills and drills Elizabeth used for Roman can be used for any toddler and preschool child to prepare them for success throughout school and all new situations they may encounter in childhood.

Elizabeth, Tom, and Roman you are an amazing, and inspiring family. I look forward with great anticipation to the next chapters of Roman's adventures.

~ **Robert Silver, MD**
Medical Director, Neonatology
Jeff Gordon Children's Hospital
Carolinas Medical Center – NorthEast
Concord, NC

Contents

Introduction

Raindrops on Roman – Overcoming Autism: A Message of Hope was written to share my journey through our son's recovery from autism. I believe this story can be a message of hope to parents of babies and toddlers who have just been given this devastating diagnosis and think that it is impossible to overcome. My goal is to provide a guideline of the therapies, treatments, and skills and drills that were instrumental in our son's recovery. (Recovery is the possibility of regaining something that was lost or returning to a normal condition.) To better enlighten the reader of what we went through, I provide anecdotes of various situations and the methods we used to help him recover. This is a testimonial of my son's recovery program and what worked for us, and I believe many parents can benefit from my story.

Autism is a developmental brain disorder that typically presents itself within the first three years of a child's life. It is a condition that adversely affects social skills, verbal and nonverbal communication, self-help, behavior, and constructive play. Children with autism exhibit similar peculiar behaviors, such as lack of eye contact, hand flapping, atypical tolerance for pain, fixation on objects or toys, repetitive behaviors, absence or loss of language, not smiling, or not answering to their name. Some children may engage in many atypical behaviors while others may have just a few. There are five disorders categorized within the autism spectrum: Autistic Disorder, Asperger's Disorder, Pervasive Developmental Disorder-Not Otherwise Specified (PDD-NOS) – which was my son's disorder – Childhood Disintegrative Disorder, and Rett's Disorder.

The cause of autism is still unknown. Doctors, scientists, and researchers have numerous theories as to what causes it, such as vaccines, environmental toxins, pesticides in foods, and Tuberculosis, but there is no known single identifiable cause. In 2007 the Center for Disease Control reported that one in every 150 children is diagnosed with autism, one in every 94 boys. It is four times more likely to occur in boys than in girls and can range from mild to severe.

At 18 months our son Roman was diagnosed with Sensory Processing Disorder (SPD). SPD means the brain is disorganized and cannot process incoming sensory information correctly, and the child misinterprets or is unable to use sensory information correctly. Roman's five senses were not functioning properly, thus making it impossible for him to interact effectively in his everyday environment.

I failed to comprehend how dire the situation was until they said the ever-petrifying "A" word – autism. When they said that he had symptoms that were under the umbrella of autism, all that I remember is a haze coming over me and teardrops making my eyes go dim. I became so lightheaded that I actually felt I was going to faint. I had never even entertained the idea that he could have autism. I thought, "This can't be happening. Not autism. They must be mistaken."

I knew what autism was because I had worked with children with autism at a camp for children with special needs when I was a teenager. He wasn't withdrawn. He had great eye contact and played well with toys. He didn't act like a child with this disorder, or so I thought. I didn't really understand what constituted autism, and they wouldn't say that he was autistic. They only said he had Pervasive Developmental Disorder, which, unbeknownst to me at the time, is autism.

Pervasive Development Disorder, or PDD, is characterized by severe, pervasive impairment in the development of all or many areas, including social interaction, verbal and nonverbal communication, and self-help. I don't quite remember what they said after that. I was devastated and instantly propelled into a state of anxiety. I had to find out what to do to stop this from happening. I was terrified at the thought that we could potentially lose our son. I believed it would be the end of the hopes and dreams we had for him. I knew we had to go to war; we had a very dangerous and frightening battle to win.

Our son received treatment from a program called Early Childhood Intervention (ECI). Fortunately for us, they provided us with the therapists he would need so we did not have to use precious time seeking out other doctors or interventions, and we used ECI services exclusively. I knew that we had to go to work immediately. Early intervention is extremely critical; everyday we delayed therapy meant that Roman would be slipping away.

It is crucial to begin intensive intervention as early as you can. The sooner you begin therapy, the better the chances for improvement. This is because the brain is considered malleable in a child from birth to age 5; it can be shaped or changed. We literally had to retrain Roman's brain; we had to teach him how to compensate for the symptoms he was experiencing due to the dysfunction in his brain. This book explains the methods and procedures we used on our son.

There are many different treatments, therapies, and interventions available, and new scientific and medical breakthroughs are occurring all the time. Parents must seek out which treatments best meet the needs of their child. Autism can be a very expensive disability. I wasn't going to return to work because I knew I had to be there to help our son. With only my husband's salary supporting us, I worried about how expensive this was going to be, but ECI is a very affordable therapy and has a family cost share system.

ECI immediately assigned Roman speech and occupational therapists. They also educate parents on how to work with their children when their therapists are not in the home. I was involved in each therapy session and they taught me which techniques and methods to use to help with each specific problem. I knew that if he were to have any chance of getting better he would have to be engaged in an intensive therapy routine. Intensive early intervention means beginning treatment and therapies as early as possible using a professionally designed, consistent therapy plan. My life was immediately transformed into a world of therapists, schedules, and treatments.

As his mother I learned that there was a lot that I could do. I had to become my child's advocate and help decide which treatments and therapies would best benefit our son. I then became "Mommy therapist." I listed all the problems he had and then created my own "skills and drills" program to facilitate his recovery process.

As a Christian and a woman of prayer, I had to rely on my strong faith in the Lord to get me through this without falling apart. I couldn't allow these overwhelming fears of losing our son to paralyze me. There is an old adage that says, "Worry looks around, sorry looks back, but faith looks up." So I focused on the biblical scripture that says, "Do not be anxious about anything, but by prayer and petition, with thanksgiving, present your requests to God." (Philippians 4:6) Every night while Roman was sleeping I literally prayed over him in his crib and asked God to heal him.

Raindrops on Roman is the story of Roman's recovery and has the 78 skills and drills I used to overcome each of his sensory and autistic problems. These skills and drills were modified for ages one through five. There are many books on the market that cover the technical and medical aspects of autism and disclose current data and therapies, but the purpose of my story is simply to share the successful techniques used in our son's recovery. What is so amazing is that God can take your painful experiences and turn them into something you can use to help others.

Every child with autism has different challenges, but I believe that with intensive early intervention there can be improvement and, in some cases, recovery. I hope this story will be a blessing to you and may provide some hope, information, and guidelines on how to go about your own child's journey through autism. Let's nurture our child's nature.

We have two natures in our breast,
One is foul, one is blessed;
One I love and one I hate,
But the one I feed will dominate.

– Author unknown

This poem so aptly fits our son because his one nature was foul, the other blessed. I fed the blessed one, and that's the nature he now has.

CHAPTER ONE

What's Wrong with My Child?

September 11, 2001. Everyone remembers what they were doing on *that* day. I was having a baby. I arrived at the hospital at 5:00 a.m. to be induced. The medicine was beginning to take effect, and the pain, I assure you, was acute. Three hours later I saw a plane crashing into the World Trade Center! I couldn't believe it. I'm having my first baby and 9/11 happens.

I should have known that this could be a foreshadowing of what was yet to follow. What should have been the happiest day of my life turned into a day of distress and sorrow. Our son was to be born that day, but I surely didn't want his birthday to be on 9/11. Even my doctor said she didn't want him born that day. I spent the rest of that day in despair, watching the horrifying events unfold before my eyes. Luckily my son had the good sense not to come yet. He waited until the early morning of September 12th to arrive.

"Congratulations! You have a healthy, beautiful baby boy!" That's what the doctors always say when a child is born with no apparent physical or mental disabilities. They never tell you about developmental problems that could occur one or two years later, so most parents have no idea what they could be in for. I was an older first-time mom, and we were ready, excited, and looking forward to the joys and challenges of parenting. Roman was a splendid baby who right from birth was very alert and aware. All was well. I had an incredible husband and baby, we had just built a marvelous home, and I was now a stay-at-home mom. Never predicting, imagining, or knowing the long and winding road we were about to go down, I thought my life was just about perfect.

Roman was a happy baby and met all of his developmental milestones up until about 15 months. He sat, rolled, smiled, babbled, crawled, and walked on time. By eight months he was sleeping straight through the night for 12 long, marvelous hours. His first year of life was enjoyable and he was everything that any parent could want in a baby.

Perhaps I should have known there was something different about our son when he seemed to have this keen sense of direction by the time he was only seven months old. When Roman was six months old I began jogging again, and I took him with me in his running stroller. Each day I ran the same three-mile route. About a month into my routine I didn't want to go the same way. When I turned to go down a different street, he began to fuss. At first I thought he wanted something to drink, but it wasn't that. I tried to continue down the different street, but he continued to cry. He didn't want me to go that way. I thought, "He can't possibly be upset because I am going a different way." Yet when I turned around to go down the street he was used to, he immediately stopped crying and was happy and smiling again. And so it continued; if I didn't run the exact route and to the specific spot where I turned around to head back home, he would cry. In less than a month he knew exactly what my running route was and was only content if I ran the same way. I, indeed, thought it was strange but then proudly said to myself, "What a smart baby."

There were two other idiosyncrasies that he had as an infant, and these were my first red flags. He didn't like for anyone to hold him except me or my husband. I was constantly being told that he was just a "mama's boy," so I didn't think too much about it. By eight months of age he didn't like for anyone to touch his head or any part of his body as a gesture of affection, and he would actually wipe off any place that someone patted him. I thought that, too, was odd.

Roman occasionally choked while nursing; this was my second red flag. It wasn't a constant thing, and I just patted him on the back and commenced feeding again. When it came time to actually feed him baby food, his choking increased. He had a difficult time swallowing and didn't like the taste of virtually anything I tried to give him. I mostly nursed the first year of his life because that was all he really wanted. I told his pediatrician my concerns and her explanation was that he was just a picky eater and when he got hungry enough, he'd eat.

After his first birthday there were definite and concrete red flags in his behavior and mannerisms which were becoming increasingly more pronounced. Roman learned to walk at 13 months and by 14 months he began running, and running, and running. He loved to go for long walks and he would end up running most of the way; he could actually run a whole mile by the time he was 15 months. Soon he began running laps around our family room, and that was my third red flag. By 15 and 16 months he was running 50 to 60 laps a day. I would have to stop him because he never got tired. What I thought was going to be the making of a potential track star was just the beginning of a much larger problem.

When I tried to introduce him to solid foods he would often choke. He didn't like to chew, so I had to cut his food into tiny little pieces. I repeatedly told his pediatrician about my concerns, but she had an answer for everything. Unfortunately, all of her answers were wrong. All three of my red flags she justified with, "He doesn't want anyone else holding him because he's a 'mama's boy,'" "He's just a picky eater," and "He's getting good exercise running around the house."

I continually told her that I thought something was wrong with my son. She finally became so frustrated with me that she actually had the audacity to say, "Why do you keep saying something's wrong with him? He's a perfectly healthy baby. Do you want something to be wrong with him? You're just an overly anxious older mom."

I was infuriated by her callousness. I told her, "Of course I don't want something to be wrong with him. How could you ask me that?" She then told me to just relax and enjoy him.

By 16 months his choking increased tremendously and he was choking almost every day. He could barely chew or swallow. My husband and I finally took him to Children's Hospital for a video swallow study because we thought there was something wrong with his esophagus, preventing him from swallowing correctly. This was just conjecture, but I knew that something wasn't right and we had to find out.

DIAGNOSIS

Upon arriving at the hospital we were fortunately greeted by a nurse who had previously worked for a program called Early Childhood Intervention. She asked me if he was a picky eater and if he didn't like to touch things. I immediately said "Yes!" She replied that he didn't need a video swallow study and told us he had a condition called Sensory Processing Disorder.

"Sensory what?" I asked. We had never heard of that. She explained that his sensory processing was atypical and that he needed Early Childhood Intervention. I also had to ask her what that was. She informed us that Early Childhood Intervention (ECI) is a state- and federally-funded government program that would provide all the types of therapies he would need. (For more information about ECI, see Appendix III.)

She also reassured us that with intervention he would be fine. That was all I needed to hear – "He would be fine." We still had no idea what this disorder was and were about to be introduced to a whole new world of language, therapists, and treatment we had never known before. Although I didn't understand the severity of his condition, I was relieved to finally have a diagnosis and was excited to get started with treatment.

At 17 months Roman's conditioned worsened. He began something called "stimming." This is an obsessive, ritualistic behavior where the child exhibits repetitive body movements or may become fixated on an object. They disconnect from the outside world by engaging in habitual and often mesmerizing activities. Roman began rolling his hands around and around, staring at ceiling fans and flags, and constantly running laps inside the family room.

Things that didn't bother him before were no longer tolerable to him. He began to hate having his hair and face washed or teeth brushed. He didn't want anything to touch his face or head. He would not put on any kind of hat or cap and was afraid to put anything around his eyes, such as play sunglasses. Then, all of a sudden, he would no longer let me take his picture or record him on the video camera. I was becoming more bewildered and thought, "He used to love having his picture taken; now he's afraid of a camera?" Even worse, his personality was changing. He used to be a happy, smiling baby but was rapidly becoming more disconcerted and irate.

At 18 months ECI came to our home and did an assessment. This is a test used to identify the child's strengths and needs, followed by an evaluation to determine what services he would require. They agreed that he indeed did have Sensory Processing Disorder (SPD). They explained that SPD occurs in the central nervous system. The brain is disorganized and cannot process incoming sensory information correctly, making it difficult for the child to behave appropriately. The child misinterprets or is unable to use sensory information in an appropriate and logical manner. SPD affects the child's learning, play, communication, behavioral, and social skills.

According to Maryann Colby Trott, as stated in *SenseAbilities: Understanding Sensory Integration*, "Our brains must be able to organize and process sensory input, and to use that input to respond appropriately to a particular situation. To do so we must integrate information we receive through all of our senses and from movement and gravity."[1]

Our five senses of sight, sound, smell, taste, and touch integrate and work together to give us the knowledge we need to function and help us live. We use many of our senses at the same time when engaging in everyday activities. Trott goes on to say, "Children must be able to take in information through all channels and perform many skills automatically. They must know and be comfortable with where their bodies are in relation to their environment; they must feel safe and know what information to pay attention to and what to ignore."[2]

SPD can affect all five senses or just a few of them. These sensory differences often make the child anxious and upset about non-threatening, harmless sensations. Because the senses allow you to function, any sensory disorder causes a child to have trouble successfully interacting in their everyday environment. Because Roman had sensory dysfunction, he did not know how to handle the different sensory input he was receiving.

They informed me that Roman's SPD affected his touch, taste, and sight. He was immediately assigned a speech therapist to help him learn to talk and an occupational therapist to help him with his touch, fine motor, and behavioral issues. Roman also qualified for a nutritionist. He had a very difficult time eating; he didn't like most foods and was extremely thin. A nutritionist helped me plan a proper, healthy diet that he could tolerate so he could gain weight and finally enjoy some food.

I hesitantly thought, "Okay, this sounds a little ominous, but we can fix this." But when they said he had Pervasive Developmental Disorder (PDD), and that was under the umbrella of autism, I was devastated. To me, the fear I felt was analogous to that of the lion on *The Wizard of Oz* when he goes before the Wizard to ask for courage. The Wizard tells the lion that he must first bring him the witch's broom. The lion is so frightened that he turns and runs down a long endless hall and jumps right through a window. That was always a classic scene to me, and right then, I was the lion.

CHAPTER TWO

What Can We Do to Help Roman?

I knew Roman was in trouble, and we were in a fight to save our son. From the time they gave me his diagnosis at 18 months, and for the next two and a half years, he had all-encompassing, intensive intervention.

Early Childhood Intervention helps babies and toddlers, ages 0-3, with disabilities or delays in their development, children who have been diagnosed with a physical or medical condition that causes a developmental delay, or children with atypical sensory problems or behavior patterns. A developmental delay is when various skills that babies and toddlers should attain by a certain age, such as crawling, talking, or eating, are not met. There can be cognitive delay, such as not following directions; speech and language delay, such as a loss of language or being non-verbal; physical delays, like crawling; fine motor delay, like building a block tower; self-help delays, like potty training; and social and emotional delays, such as learning how to play and interact appropriately with others.

One of the many great things about this service is that the therapists come to your home, day-care, or home-care setting, and you can be there to assist and learn the various intervention techniques. They want to work with you in the child's most natural environment, meaning where he plays, eats, gets dressed, or potty trains. ECI also provides a myriad of other therapists, including a psychologist, nutritionist, and nurse, and does vision and hearing assessments. Every parent must make the decision as to what they believe will be the right treatment for their child, but you should consider the recommendations of your doctor or the professionals who diagnosed and evaluated your child.

ECI was the only program we used. Roman's occupational and speech therapists taught me the strategies he needed to overcome his sensory and autistic behaviors. They showed me what to do for him, and I carried it out throughout the day; that is the key to helping your child on his way to recovery.

SKILLS AND DRILLS

I called the therapists I would be working with to establish a treatment program. The ECI therapists and I collaborated and planned developmentally appropriate educational activities with identified behavioral and learning objectives according to his age developmental level and specific needs. He received functional spontaneous communication, organized language skills, cognitive development, play skills, and behavioral modification skills. Also included were standardized monthly evaluations that targeted specific areas of Roman's skills and abilities along with monthly team meetings to monitor and measure his progress and provide feedback.

The therapy sessions and a skills and drills program I put together combined language and academic skills, and sensory motor experiences, including tactile, oral, visual, vestibular, and proprioceptive skills. Roman received speech therapy once a week for an hour and occupational therapy twice a week for an hour. I knew that was not going to be enough, so they advised me on what I needed to do, and then I implemented my own game plan. As a former elementary teacher, I instinctively used my teaching and classroom skills and applied them to my son. I created and developed my own in-home intervention program to successfully apply the skills needed to change Roman's behavior.

By the time he was 22 months, Roman had developed more autistic and sensory problems. Some were severe; others were less acute. I had a checklist of 45 things that were wrong with him, and I had to undo and correct all 45 problems. Everything that he was afraid of and didn't want to do was exactly what we had to make him do. The question was, "How are we going to accomplish this enormous task?"

I purchased all the supplies and toys he would need and rearranged our family and game rooms to create my own in-home therapy center. I set up small learning centers (which were two small tables and a few play areas) that I called "stations." I had different stations to deal with the various sensory issues he had. Each one had a different activity related to the things he was afraid to do and would not do. These skills and drills taught him how to learn and play in an appropriate and meaningful way.

I had a station for touching textured objects, a station for arts and crafts, a station for strengthening fine and gross motor control, and a station for speech, reading, and puzzles. I had skills and drills for every problem we had to correct. He had to complete five to ten minutes on an activity before moving on to the next one. We did a lot of sensory processing therapy to improve the way the brain processes and organizes sensations. He had to touch and feel things he was frightened of and immerse himself in all of the activities he didn't want to do. I had him repeat each skill over and over again because I knew that repetition is critical for the brain to process new behaviors and skills and is essential to re-training the brain.

If he resisted doing an activity, I implemented a two-minute time-out and then made him finish it. Over time he stopped resisting and completed all the activities, but I had to be consistent. With every activity I always encouraged him to say words in order to increase his speech. I also taught him how to clean up after each activity before we began a different one. I monitored his progress weekly through charts so I could modify and increase treatments to meet all of his specific needs. I was compelled to work with him ten hours a day, everyday, and I was relentless. The ten hours did include meal times, day trips, and basic skills used in normal everyday activities. Our intensive treatment included 56 hours of the main treatment foundation I called the skills and drills, 12 hours of preschool, one hour of professional speech therapy, and two hours of professional occupational therapy each week.

THE RIGHT PEDIATRICIAN

The Early Intervention therapists asked me why it took me so long to figure out that something was wrong with Roman. I told them that his pediatrician assured us he was perfectly healthy and that there was nothing to worry about. They advised me to find another pediatrician that knew about sensory issues and were able to actually give me information about a pediatrician that was adept in this area. Roman's new pediatrician was fantastic and completely understood his issues and everything he was going through. She was patient and empathetic and knew how to handle his fears. She even offered many ideas on how to handle certain situations.

One major reason that babies are getting diagnosed so late is because many pediatricians do not know all the different signs related to autism, and many have never even heard of Sensory Processing Disorder. This is extremely detrimental and parents lose critical time getting help for their babies when they go undiagnosed for so long. I told his former pediatrician about his diagnosis of Sensory Processing Disorder, and she told me she had never even heard of it. Had the previous pediatrician known about SPD, we may have recognized the red flags earlier. His autism might not have become so pervasive because we would have started intervention when he was younger. By her not knowing the signs for autism, I lost a good nine months from when he began showing the three red flags until he was diagnosed.

Due to the fact that autism is escalating so quickly today, I believe that every mother with a newborn should be given a developmental checklist at the baby's first month check-up and told what autism warning signs to watch out for. Some autistic behaviors could show up in the first three to six months of a baby's life, at which time a parent can request early intervention and begin tackling these issues before the behaviors cause more pervasive developmental problems. (For more on this subject, see Appendix IV.)

CHAPTER THREE

Ron Burton Training Village

Once we determined all of Roman's issues, we had to try and defeat the multitude of sensory and autistic problems he had. I remember making the dreaded phone call home to my parents to tell them his diagnosis. It was even more heartbreaking because at the time my father was dying of bone cancer and had only a few more months to live. Bone cancer is an excruciatingly painful cancer and he had suffered immensely. He was a man of great faith, and, while struggling to take each breath, he whispered to me, "Just pray, Elizabeth, pray that God heals him." I couldn't believe the trial I had to endure, and I had to rely on the Lord for my strength. Beginning that night I began a prayer vigil for a healing for our son.

When he was 19 months, I initiated my skills and drills program, and he began doing all the various stations. After just three months, I had to take a hiatus from the program in order to go to my parent's home in Boston to help my father. My family runs a non-profit, summer sports camp for underprivileged inner city youth in rural Massachusetts called the Ron Burton Training Village. My father, Ron Burton, was a former Boston Patriot and he started the camp 24 years ago as a way to give back to the community. Every summer, in July, my husband and I went up to work at the camp.

Since Roman had only had a few months of therapy, I wanted to stay home. I knew that he should not miss any skills and drills and therapy sessions, but my dad was dying and this would be my last time to see him and work with him at his camp. The therapists understood my dilemma and reassured me that too much time would not be lost, and we would resume therapy when we returned.

I hadn't seen my family in almost a year, and they were dismayed and discouraged to see how much Roman had changed. They had last seen him at Christmas when he was 15 months, but now, at 22 months, his regression was quite apparent. I tried to explain what we were dealing with, but they didn't really understand. I didn't fault them because I didn't understand it all yet either.

When we first arrived, they saw how Roman wouldn't let anyone touch him and did not want anyone greeting him. My eldest brother thoughtlessly asked, "Why is he so afraid of everyone and so attached to you? You need to stop babying him and toughen him up."

I couldn't believe what a nerve it struck in me and I immediately went on the defense and angrily yelled, "He's got Sensory Processing Disorder! He can't help it! How dare you be so callous?" My brother looked at me like I was crazy, but he probably just thought I was being my usual temperamental self. I know he didn't mean to be insensitive. It was so painful for me to see how people reacted to his behavior, but it was even more painful to know that Roman was trapped inside his mind and couldn't get out.

While we were away at camp, Roman began to get worse. He was rapidly developing more autistic-like traits, such as repetitive movements and obsessive behaviors. I attempted to do some skills and drills, but I wasn't able to be consistent or establish a good schedule. I was too busy working at camp and trying to help my father.

Each day there seemed to be a new issue that was bothering Roman. He began lashing out and screaming if anyone approached just to touch him and say hello. He began to repeatedly yell "Aaah" for no reason at all. It was embarrassing and frustrating. The campers just looked at him like he was crazy. Some of my friends were appalled and thought he was belligerent. I told them he had Sensory Processing Disorder and tried to explain why he behaved this way, but they didn't fully understand either.

On the other hand, one saving grace was my mother; she was the one person that he was never afraid of and truly enjoyed. I relied on her a lot for guidance and support. She always encouraged me to keep working with him, but she, too, was apprehensive. One day when we were shopping at the store, we were waiting in an unusually long checkout line. The whole time Roman just stared at the ceiling fan and refused to take his eyes off of it. It was then that my mother forlornly confessed, "I don't know, Elizabeth. I think he's in trouble."

"So do I," I replied, brokenhearted.

A FATHER'S PLIGHT

That summer we had a family friend, who was a professional athlete, come and share a very unusual story with our campers. He told them about all his successes in life. I remember him telling the young men about his athletic achievements in high school, college, and the pros, and that virtually everything he wanted in life he had achieved, except for one thing. He has a son with autism. My heart jumped. I couldn't believe the coincidence.

He was eloquent in his speech, and you couldn't help seeing his pain as he spoke of his beloved son. He said, "I've been very successful in my career and made millions of dollars, but I would gladly give away every penny just to have our son be in good health." Autism is not measured on the spectrum of wealth and poverty.

He continued, "Everyone has a cross to bear and this one is mine." The entire time he spoke, I watched Roman standing on a step, staring at a flag. I was overcome with grief and began to cry for my friend, his son, Roman, and myself. I prayed, "Please God, do not let him become autistic," not knowing he already was.

Camp was devastating that year, watching my dad slowly die right before me and watching my son slowly slip away into a world of autism. I am so thankful for my strong faith in God, because it was in those times of despair that I needed Him the most. I kept praying for wisdom and guidance, and it was the Lord who gave me the strength to stay strong. I really didn't know what was going to happen. I didn't know if God was going to help him recover, nor did I have any idea if what we were about to embark on was even going to work. I have to admit that I was scared for his life. When camp was over, my only mission was to save our son. I was going to do whatever was necessary and work as long and as hard as I could to help him recover.

After arriving home I was able to implement the skills and drills for one solid month, and then, sadly, the day after Roman's second birthday, my father passed away. We returned to Boston for the funeral, and taking him back out of his environment a second time only set him back again. The week we were there for Dad's funeral Roman was inconsolable. He cried continuously and felt frazzled and disoriented. At the funeral Roman was so hysterical and distressed that his caretaker came to get us during the service because she could not console him. Tom had to leave to go calm him down right before I was to give part of the eulogy. After the funeral I wanted to stay longer to comfort my mom, but that was out of the question. I didn't even have time to mourn the passing of my father.

We had to return home and get him back on his schedule. I knew that if I didn't do something right away and do something extreme, we were going to lose him. I told my family that I would not be coming back to Boston or to camp until Roman was healed. I also knew that if he didn't overcome this, I would never be able to work at our camp again because Roman would have to be in his own special-needs camp or summer program. Our camp was not for his age level and was not appropriate for kids with his disability. I didn't know when I would see my family again or when I would ever be back.

When we returned home I immediately restarted my skills and drills program. I bought all the supplies he needed and began our strict schedule. We worked from 6:30 in the morning until 7:00 at night.

CHAPTER FOUR

Roman's Autistic/Sensory Checklist

utism and Sensory Processing Disorder affect a child's overall development. According to Partners in GOALS, sensory processing "deals with accommodation, awareness, tolerance, discrimination, and organization of touch, movement, and auditory and olfactory stimuli."[3]

Three out of the five of Roman's senses were adversely affected; he also had many behavioral and emotional problems. The following is a checklist of everything that was difficult for him. A child may exhibit many or only a few of these characteristics. Roman had all of the problems listed below:

Touch (Tactile): "To bring a body part into contact with something."[4] Roman had the propensity to react negatively and emotionally to unanticipated light or firm touch sensations. He was extremely tactile defensive to light touch.

1. Peculiar need to touch certain textures and surfaces of objects

2. Repeatedly rolled his hands

3. Opened and shut his fists

4. Misinterpreted a friendly touch or hug as threatening

5. Did not like anyone to touch him except Mommy and Daddy

6. Did not like to get his hands or body messy

7. Did not like to get his face or ears washed

8. Did not like to get his teeth brushed

9. Afraid to take a shower (did not like the water coming down on his head)

10. Did not like to get his fingernails or toenails cut

11. Did not like to get his hair cut

12. Did not like to get his picture taken (this started at 18 months)

13. Extremely ticklish

14. Oversensitive to pain

15. Fine motor difficulties: feeding himself, holding a crayon, writing, buttoning

16. Afraid to touch everyday objects, such as bubbles, play dough, finger paint, shaving cream, marbles, beans, noodles

17. Afraid to go down the slide and go through tunnels at the playground

Taste (Gustatory): "To ascertain the flavor of by taking a little into the mouth."[5] Roman's taste buds were not receiving or were receiving too strongly the essential sensory information needed to taste and determine temperature for different food textures. Difficulties with taste caused oral motor problems, including chewing difficulties.

18. Difficulty chewing and swallowing

19. Excessive choking on small pieces of food

20. Extremely picky eater

21. Aversion to textures of most common, easy foods babies love, such as mashed potatoes, yogurt, pudding, Jell-O, oatmeal, eggs, toast, pancakes

22. Refused to try or taste most foods

Sight (Visual): "Something that is seen; the process, power, or functioning of seeing."[6] Roman could see up-close and faraway, and could determine one object amongst many. (Example: Seeing a red ball in a pile of blue balls)

23. Sought visual stimulation by fixating on ceiling fans, waving flags, chandeliers, things that spin

24. Extremely visual: can see things most people don't even notice

25. Constantly turned light switches on and off

26. Tremendously focused and excited by Christmas lights

Sound (Auditory): "The sensation produced by stimulation of the organs of hearing by vibrations transmitted through the air or other medium."[7]

Roman does have excellent hearing, understanding, listening, and auditory discrimination skills.

Smell (Olfactory): "To perceive the odor or scent through stimuli affecting the olfactory nerves."[8] Roman had no problems here. Very sensitive to and keen awareness of all smells (loves to smell scents, perfumes, and aroma of things).

Speech: The communication or expression of thoughts in spoken words.

27. Could not talk

28. Echolalia: Sometimes repeated words, phrases, or statements at inappropriate times

Social/Emotional: Social: Interacting with others appropriately. Emotional: Displaying the appropriate emotional response for the situation. (Example: Happy at a birthday party) Roman had a multitude of social and emotional problems.

29. Separation anxiety: very fearful and clingy to Mom

30. Overly sensitive to change

31. Overly anxious and fearful in some non-threatening situations

32. Extremely literal

33. Easily frustrated when playing with other children

34. Very cautious: when told not to touch something, he wouldn't touch it. I didn't have to baby-proof our house.

35. Very sensitive to the feelings of others; didn't like any unkind words said or mean things done to anyone

36. Very active and fidgety

37. Loved to run laps around the house

38. Could not sit still

39. Not aggressive

40. Not a risk taker

41. Never got hurt because he set up his own boundaries while playing

Behavioral: The manner of conducting oneself; the response of an individual to its environment. Roman had many behavioral problems.

42. Difficulty transitioning from one place or activity to another; had to tell him in advance and then count down when we were leaving or ending an activity

43. Difficulty tolerating changes in plans or expectations of an event

Organizational: The state of being neat and organized. Roman was methodical and extremely neat.

44. Constantly lined up certain toys and objects

45. Overly organized and neat with his toys

CHAPTER FIVE

Skills and Drills:
Purpose and Methodology

As a former elementary teacher, I was able to put together an efficient and developmentally appropriate skills and drills program. I used the same teaching techniques that I used in the classroom and modified the curriculum for toddler and pre-kindergarten. My professional teaching experience gave me the confidence I needed to proceed with my own program. The good news is that it does not require a college degree to teach the skills and drills or any part of your own chosen personal intervention. But it does require dedication! Along with a family's own professional treatments and interventions, parents can implement their own supplemental therapy by creating a personalized program that fits their schedules and targets their child's specific needs.

The purpose of my skills and drills was to help Roman overcome autistic behaviors through appropriate, meaningful play. Each skill and drill was designed to achieve a specific goal. I had to increase his attention span, eliminate the stimming and inappropriate sensory behaviors, and teach him to be focused, follow directions, and play correctly with toys. I performed a variety of drills to facilitate with language, fine and gross motor skills, and behavioral problems. I then implemented my own methodology, which I called the "C-R-S

Plan": Consistency, Repetition, and Structure. In order for there to be improvement, I had to apply these three things. The skills and drills must be done with consistency, meaning everyday. They need to be repetitive; repeat the skills over and over again until mastered. And they should be done in a structured and familiar environment, such as a home or preschool setting.

Another critical step towards recovery and improvement is a schedule. Roman had to have predictability and normalcy. It was mandatory that I adhered to a daily schedule so he knew what to anticipate and what was expected of him, and it had to be carried out in an organized and logical manner. This consistency gave him security and confidence. The following is a time line of Roman's daily schedule from 18 months until age four.

7:00: Wake up/get dressed

7:30: Breakfast

8:00-8:30: Table-time skills

8:30-9:00: Floor-time skills

9:00-9:30: Table-time skills

9:30-10:00: Floor-time skills

10:00: Mid-morning snack (crackers, goldfish, fruit snacks, etc.)

10-11:30: Transition from table to floor-time skills

11:30-12:00: Lunch

12:00-1:30: Nap time (can take longer or shorter nap time)

1:30-2:00: Floor-time skills (exercise drills)

2:00-2:30: Table-time skills

3:00: Snack

3:00-4:30: "Park therapy" (at a playground or park)

4:30-5:30: Transition from table to floor-time skills

5:30-6:00: Dinner

6:00-6:30: Reading time

7:00: Bathtub play

7:30: Bedtime

From age two and a half to four, Roman had preschool from 9:00 a.m.-2:00 p.m. on Tuesday and Thursday. From age three to four, he had speech therapy from 8:30-10:30 a.m. on Monday and Wednesday. When he came home from school, we worked on more skills and drills until bedtime.

An outline and summary of the execution of all the activities is in Appendix II: Skills and Drills Lessons. The skills taught correct and appropriate play and early preschool curriculum and concepts. With each activity I incorporated lots of language skills. I encouraged him to pronounce words or at least a beginning consonant sound. I always modeled the skill first so he knew what he was supposed to do and how to do it correctly, because a behavior is more likely to be learned when an example is provided.

The drills were designed to help him memorize and master specific skills. All of the skill and drills I did with Roman addressed something he was afraid of or couldn't do. It was imperative that he learned how to overcome his irrational fears, master certain objectives, and play appropriately, because these are all things that children do at school and in their homes. He would not be able to participate in a regular classroom if he did not overcome his fears.

The technique we used to get him over his fears was to have him repeatedly engage in everything he was afraid to do in order for him to see that there was nothing to fear. For example, Roman was afraid of finger paint, so I took a little dab and put it on my finger and then put a little on his finger. Then I took his finger and had him touch the paint. I did a little at a time. When he saw that it was safe, he put more fingers in it, then his hands. In the beginning he cried, so I washed it off and tried again. I did this everyday for about five minutes until he began to feel comfortable. In about two weeks he was actually finger painting with different colored paints and enjoying it. I put paint on his arms and legs and he was no longer afraid. I continued the same process with all the textures that he was afraid of. Once he began touching different textures, it desensitized him and he began to play and enjoy them.

There are skills and drills for table time and floor time. It was important that Roman learned to sit at a table. When a child goes to preschool, they are expected to be able to sit and attend for a small amount of time. I had Roman switch from table to floor so he was not sitting too long in one place. Playing on the floor is great for babies and toddlers because you are at eye level with them. Even with the C-R-S methodology, it still took a while for him to accomplish and master our objectives, but I refused to give up.

MEEP APPROACH

There were four steps I always did to help Roman overcome his fears. I call it the "MEEP" approach: 1) Model, 2) Engage, 3) Encourage, 4) Praise. Model what you want him to do. Help him engage in the activity, and do not allow him to quit. Encourage him to do it. Give lots of praise, cheers, and rewards at the end. This will encourage him to keep doing it and hopefully overcome the problem.

SETTING

All therapies should be carried out in a safe, comfortable, and natural environment like the home or preschool where the child lives, learns, and plays. I had a small table and chair for him to sit at to complete the assigned tasks. The table was important for getting him to sit and attend to the specific skill. I also had designated areas on the rug where I did floor-time skills. I interchanged between table tasks and floor fun.

When we first began, he spent only a few minutes on each task. To better facilitate this process I used a timer. I set the timer for one or two minutes and explained to him that he must sit and do the skill until the timer went off. As his attention span increased over the weeks and months, I was able to lengthen the amount of time we spent on each skill and drill. In the beginning, Roman could only sit for about 30 seconds before he would bolt out of his chair and want to run, and this was when I had to implement the infamous "time-out."

TIME-OUT

Every parent should use the discipline technique that they feel works best for their child. For me, it was the time-out method. In the first year of our program, time-out was essential in order to accomplish the skills and drills because Roman didn't want to do them. He would resist, oppose, defy, and cry, and I had to develop a thick skin and make him go to time-out when he refused to do what I said. I had a designated area in the corner wall in the dining room that I used for time-out. I had him either sit on a mat, a chair, or on the floor. He would immediately begin to cry, and I always had to stand over him to make him stay.

Time-out should be done according to a child's age; again, use a timer or stop watch. If he's one year old, he stays in one minute. If he's two years old, he sits for two minutes, and so on. However, if they are upset and need longer to calm down, they can stay longer. This was a painful process for him and me, but it worked. I had to be consistent and not give in. When the time was up I made him return and complete the assigned activity. When he refused, he had to go back to time-out.

I had to put Roman in time-out eleven times in one day. He cried each time. That was what I considered a real bad day. By the eighth time I was crying, too. But when he finally returned to the table, he completed the task. It was almost like I had to break his resistance. He had to learn that I was not going to give in. I had to be firm and do it with love.

Time-out only worked if I remained calm and in control. There was light at the end of the proverbial tunnel over time as he got used to the activities and began to enjoy doing the skills. As I mentioned, when we first began, Roman could literally sit for only about 30 seconds, but by the time he was three, he could sit for an hour doing various skills, drills, and play.

Another thing Roman needed me to do is called "hand-overhand." Whatever skills and drills he was unwilling or afraid to do, I helped him with my hand over his hand. I placed my hand over his and guided him through the specific task until he felt comfortable. I had to do hand-over-hand on most of the activities when I first began. This was effective because he trusted me and therefore was not as fearful of what I was doing with him. This allowed him to be able to complete the task. As he began to feel more secure, I had him do it himself. Even when he had difficulty accomplishing a task, I kept encouraging him with lots of praise.

PRAISE AWAY!

Praise, praise, and praise again! It was equally imperative that I gave him lots of praise when doing the skills and drills. He tried harder when he knew he was pleasing me, and it made him feel good that he was accomplishing something. I always made sure to praise and commend him for even trying the skills, because many of the tasks were very difficult for him. Remember, his brain was saying one thing, and I was telling him to do another. He always knew how proud I was of him for trying each skill, even when I had to put him in time-out five times before he would do it. So praise away!

STIMMING

Many children with autism do something called stimming. This self-stimulatory behavior reduces sensory overload and/or can stimulate their senses. They engage in repetitive body movements involving any of the five senses, including behaviors such as staring at or fixating on objects like ceiling fans and lights, opening and closing fists, moving fingers in front of their face, hand flapping or waving, lining up objects, running around in circles, rocking back and forth, shrieking or yelling out, echolalia, and smelling or licking different objects.

When Roman stared at flags or fans, I told him, "Please don't stare at the fan. Let's build blocks." I redirected him to a fun activity in order to stop the staring. I always redirected and rewarded with praise. Whenever he began to stim, I had a three-step strategy. I warned him to stop, did a count down, and replaced the behavior with something else, such as a toy, or began clapping or singing in order to distract and redirect him. I would say, "You can run five more laps around the room," or "You can roll your hand for ten more seconds," and then counted from one to ten. I had to have a countdown because if I were to end it abruptly, the undesirable behaviors only increased. Since I didn't know when he would begin to stim, I had to constantly be on watch, ready to redirect.

Many times throughout the day I had to stop Roman from rolling his hands around and opening and closing his fists. I would take his hands, look him in the eye, and say, "No more rolling your hands." After the countdown, I replaced that movement with an appropriate activity, such as playing with a soft stretch-and-squeeze toy or ball. Hand-fidgets are effective toys to help an over-stimulated child calm down and refocus.

He often cried because he wanted to stim, but I refused to allow him to do it. Every time he stimmed, I stopped, redirected, and replaced it with something else. I also had an adequate supply of replacement toys, such as squeeze toys, beanbags, soft squishy balls, and sponges that I placed in his hands when he began to stim. Stimming can happen at any time and this task was extremely tedious and exhausting, but I looked at this struggle as a means to an end. Eventually the stimming began to diminish and then completely went away.

Roman liked to yell "Aaah" for no reason and at the most inappropriate times. I told him he could not yell "Aaah" anymore but to say "A," and then I redirected him and commenced singing the alphabet song, beginning with the letter "A."

Over the months I noticed that he wasn't rolling his hands anymore. He was no longer running laps in the house or staring at ceiling fans and lights. He no longer yelled "Aaah!" Instead I was yelling "Aaah-Alleluia!" I honestly couldn't believe it. These techniques were actually working! Roman had at least seven different stimming rituals, and they *all* stopped. What is so incredible about this is that once he stopped them, they stopped for good; he didn't revert to those stimming behaviors again.

RESULTS

A few months into my intensive in-home skills and drills program, I began to see results. They weren't immediate, but I could see improvement in many of the drills we were working on in a reasonable amount of time. This gave me the incentive to keep going. Most of his stimming went away first, which was extremely encouraging and gave me so much hope for beating this. I began checking off many of the problems Roman needed to overcome.

Because we maintained such a strict schedule, I could see that the C-R-S method was working. He knew what to expect and was becoming less fearful of objects. Roman was able to sit for longer periods of time and was able to accomplish each skill. The skills and drills were becoming more familiar and he was beginning to have mastery in almost every area. I was absolutely thrilled and encouraged with what was unfolding right before my eyes.

Because he began having a fear of cameras, I have no pictures of Roman from 18 months until two years and three months. After doing our camera drills, I was finally able to take his picture again in time for his Christmas card photo. Friends complimented Roman and said how much they loved his picture. (If they only knew what it took for me to finally get him to smile for a camera again.)

CHAPTER SIX

Mother's Role

I know that most mothers have to work outside the home, and, as a former teacher, I had also planned to return to work. But when Roman was diagnosed I knew that it was vital and prudent that I not do so. I knew I had to be an advocate and intercede on behalf of our son. I had to gather all of life's lessons and then tackle autism head-on, right where it originated. It was a daunting task, but it was up to me to be actively involved on a daily basis if he was going to have any chance of getting better.

Early Intervention came only twice a week for three hours and that wasn't near enough time to get a child well. They gave me the knowledge of what to do, and I had to carry out these tasks all day, everyday. Autism can be an extremely expensive disability. There are many wonderful methods, treatments, clinics, and private therapies. Private schools for children with autism can cost anywhere from $15,000 to $100,000 a year, and most are not covered by insurance. (Parents are fighting for laws requiring states to provide health insurance coverage for intensive and extremely costly therapies for autism. Six states have passed these laws for coverage to be enacted in 2008 and 2009; forty-four more still to go.)

We couldn't afford these expensive private therapies and

schools. Many children with autism need a lot of one-on-one therapy, so if he was going to get better, I had to do it. I considered this to be an investment in our child's life, and the return was immeasurable. I helped give our son his life back, and there is no amount of money one can make in the workforce that could ever make up for that. If I hadn't at least tried and made a concerted effort, he may not have ever recovered, and I would have had to spend endless amounts of money on the private therapies and treatments he would have needed for many years to come.

What was so great about working with the Roman was that he responded very well to me. He knows, loves, and trusts me, and wanted so much to please me, even when frustrated and having tantrums. He couldn't help how he was, but I had to help him help himself. I must admit that this was very overwhelming and was definitely the most difficult thing I have ever done. In order to take on this enormous task, a mother has to develop a new mindset. You have to approach this as your job, your new purpose in life. Please remember that it's only for a "season," a period of two, three, or even four years of complete dedication to your child's well-being in an attempt to reclaim or improve his life. I believe that if I had put my son in day-care and didn't put in the time helping him, he never would have overcome all of his autistic behaviors.

I also want to impart that I had many great days and enjoyable times doing the skills and drills. Once we became consistent with the program, Roman rapidly began overcoming many of his problems; I could see the improvement and results in many areas rather quickly. Because all the activities are child-centered and fun, he began to like doing the activities and looked forward to the skills and drills program.

Remember, there is only a small window of opportunity here. Doctors maintain that the most effective intervention, providing the greatest chance of full recovery, must be done before age five while the brain is still malleable. After age five there can still be significant improvement, but it is so much more difficult because the brain is less malleable.

With only one income we had to budget and cut back. We didn't take any trips or have extra money for fancy things, but we now have a completely healthy son who is doing absolutely awesome! How much is that worth? What you earn in healing him is worth more than any amount of money you could ever make. If you want to be successful in anything, you must be willing to pay the price; real success requires some kind of sacrifice.

Another unbelievable part of my story is that it didn't cost us anything for his therapies or skills and drills. The only money we ever spent was for his toys and supplies, which I figured to be about $800 over the two and a half years. And now that our child is recovered, I am free to return to the workplace if I choose to do so. I believe the two- to four-year leave of absence a mother may have to take is well worth it for a lifetime of happiness.

FRUSTRATION FACTOR

I have to admit that I had a great many frustrating days, and there were days, even weeks, that I just wanted to give up. I allowed myself to cry and feel discouraged because it took so much time and energy to break through to him. Roman could be very obstinate and belligerent. It was important that I took time for myself each day. Even though we worked ten hours a day, I still took an hour each day to run, take a long bubble bath, go out for coffee, or just go to Wal-Mart. You know you have hit a new low when you're excited to get out of the house just to go to Wal-Mart, but you have to get away to rejuvenate. I had to clear my mind and have some peace and quiet. When I failed to do this, I experienced what I call "The Frustration Factor." Those were days that were just harder than others and little things bothered me.

One day when Roman had just turned two, I took him to the park for a play-date with a girl that was four months younger than him. The mom didn't know Roman's issues yet and said, "Listen to my little Susie sing *Frére Jacques*." She sang it beautifully, even pronouncing all the French words to perfection. Instead of being happy, I was hurt. This little girl was 20 months old and singing

51

Frére Jacques, and my son couldn't even say "Mama." Woe is me!

I angrily thought to myself, "What does that song mean anyway?" while I tried my best to muster up, "Nice singing, Susie." Her proud mother then asked Roman if he would like to sing, too.

I had to answer for him, "Ah, no."

There were many months that I functioned in a state of anxiety because I so wanted him to get better, and I knew we were under a time frame. There were some days that I was truly frazzled. I remember one day in particular when I went to a Sam's Club grocery store. I was going to get some great $30 steaks to grill for a much-needed treat for my husband Tom and myself. The only reason I went there was to get the steaks, so there was literally only one thing in my basket – the steaks. I am embarrassed to tell you this story, but I have to let you know about the frustration factor.

While in Sam's, Roman had a mini-meltdown and continued throwing himself backward in the grocery cart. I was standing in a long checkout line and all the people around me were looking at him, and then at me, wondering why I couldn't get him to calm down. I tried to get him to stop but to no avail. I was embarrassed and disgusted with him and left the store as soon as I paid for my *one* item. I pulled him out of the basket, put him in the car seat, and drove off with tears in my eyes.

When I got home, I took Roman out of the car and went to get the yummy, luscious steaks that I so had a taste for, but, much to my dismay, they weren't there! I said to myself, "Where on God's good earth are the steaks? Did they fall on the car floor? No. Please let me have put them in the trunk. No, that's too much like right." I slowly closed my eyes and leaned back against the car knowing that *I had left them in the basket!!* I just couldn't believe it!

When I went into the house, Tom commented how he couldn't wait to have the steaks. I angrily told him he was going to have to wait because I hadn't gotten them yet. He said, "I thought you just went to get them." I just looked at him and told him I would be back soon. I refused to tell him that I left the one and only thing I purchased in the store's parking lot. He would have had me committed.

I left Roman with him and went back to the store, which was a good 20 minutes from my house. The basket, of course, was gone and so were the steaks. I asked the lady at the service desk if some good, honest person had returned the $30 steaks. She said, "Ah, no."

I thought, "Humph!" Even if they did, she would have probably hid them under her desk and taken them home for her own dinner.

Well, needless to say, $60 dollars later I had my new steaks. I just chalked up this negative experience to knowing that I unwillingly paid for someone else's barbeque dinner; I hope they enjoyed it. That's what I mean by the frustration factor. All of this continuous work does get to you after a while.

MARRIAGE

There is a higher divorce rate among marriages with a child with special needs due to all the stress, disappointments, and challenges. You are constantly functioning in a crisis situation. I believe that you must make it a goal to work together and communicate in order to successfully keep the marriage intact. I am fortunate to have a very patient and loving husband, Tom, who listened and valued my advice and that of the therapists. He promised to do whatever we needed him to do and was an incredible source of strength for me during this entire trial.

When we received Roman's diagnosis, we agreed that we were going to work through this together as a team. Not all fathers may be this patient, but I believe his dedication to his son was due to the fact that his father abandoned him as a baby. He vowed that he would never do that to his son because he knew how difficult life had been for him. Even though frustration, anger, and utter exhaustion completely overwhelmed us at times, we continued to communicate our feelings, fears, and discouragements. We allowed ourselves to sometimes feel defeated, but then encouraged each other and focused on the goals we had for our son.

Although Tom wasn't in the "trenches" trying to make him do all of the daily skills and drills, he spent all of his free time with Roman either before or after work. Everyday when I needed to take a break, he would either take him to the library, the park, riding on his tricycle, or for long walks around the block. We didn't have any extended family members living in our state, so it was truly only the two of us doing this task. It is imperative to enlist your spouse, parent, babysitter, or a designated competent, trustworthy friend to give you a short break during the day or evening so you can take some time for yourself.

Many states offer free respite services (or ask for a minimal payment on a sliding scale) for anyone whose child is diagnosed with a disability. Respite care is temporary care that allows the parents or the primary caretaker to take a break. It is a nice, safe way to get help and have some of the financial burden taken away. Respite care screens all the babysitters, who are usually women that are interested in caring for children with special needs. An assigned babysitter takes care of the child for several hours each week, depending upon the amount of time the family qualifies for.

Although we did not enlist any babysitters, it was equally important for Tom and I to make time for each other. I put Roman to bed every night at 7:30, and this was our opportunity to spend quiet evenings together and focus on the two of us.

There were definite "breaking point" moments when we felt like we were at our wits' end, and when one of us was not in agreement on how to handle a situation, we would have our own time-outs to regroup and discuss different strategies for solving a problem. When one of us became irritated and yelled at Roman (which 90% of the time was me), we learned how to disarm and calm each other.

Tom was inordinately patient with him, but there were a few things that Roman did that would just send him reeling. When Roman was two, he suddenly had the urge to hit our big-screen television. (Thankfully, this was before the flat-screen era, because the big-screens were more durable.) For several months, when he woke up he automatically began fussing for no apparent reason. Then he would run to the television and smack the screen with his open hand. Tom or I would try to stop him, but at some point in the day, that television was going to get hit.

Tom would yell and put him in time-out. It was as if something triggered Roman and he was not content unless he hit that television. Every morning when he woke up, one of us had to block it, and Tom was convinced he was going to break it. We repeatedly tried various techniques to make him stop hitting the TV. After finally persuading him to hit a pillow, the wall, or some other less valuable or breakable object, he finally renounced that bad habit. I will say the television lasted another two years, but after all the hits it took, it finally broke. The good news for my husband was that he used it as an excuse to purchase a new flat-screen that was now on the market. He said that he had earned it after all that he had to put up with; I had to concur.

Working together through all this actually strengthened our marriage. We respected each other's daily commitment and determination to work through this crisis. It gave us a whole new understanding of the marriage vows we took: "We will stand by each other in sickness and in health."

CHAPTER SEVEN

Tactile and Speech Challenges

One major problem that Roman had to overcome was his tactile defensiveness. Tactile defensiveness is an undesirable response to a neutral sensation. He was afraid to touch certain things and fearful of anyone reaching out to touch him. The sensory checklist describes all of the problems Roman had with touch.

Maryann Colby Trott states,

"The tactile system is our sense of touch. It is through the tactile system that we first receive information about the world through two systems called the discriminative and the protective. The discriminative system allows us to determine where we are being touched and what is touching us. The protective system tells us when we are in contact with something dangerous and causes a flight or fright response."[9]

These two systems must work together and correctly process the information received. They are crucial for interpretation of information and for survival. The defensiveness occurs when these systems are not in balance and the brain is unable to regulate these sensations. A child who experiences tactile defensiveness may demonstrate a negative response to light touch and certain textures, food, or surfaces. Being near or actually touching him may elicit undesirable behavior(s). The ability to process tactile sensations effectively is very important for visual perception, motor planning, and body awareness, as well as for academic learning, emotional security, and social skills.

Hyper-Hypo-Sensitivity

Because of his tactile defensiveness, Roman experienced hypersensitivity, or being overly responsive to touch. The brain of a child with autism may be unable to regulate sensations, and the child may avoid them because he cannot tolerate them. A child who is hypersensitive may be more anxious, cautious, or disruptive. He may scream, withdraw, or run away from objects, people, or situations he considers to be a threat. The child may focus on or become fixated, frightened, or preoccupied by meaningless and non-threatening objects or situations. He is not a risk-taker and will often steer away from the fun activities typical children do, like spinning around in circles, jumping, climbing, or swinging from a jungle gym. As a result, I never had to baby-proof my home because Roman was so cautious. If I warned him not to touch something, he would not touch it. This also afforded me the opportunity to keep him in his crib until he was three and outgrew it. Roman would never even attempt to climb out of it.

The opposite of hypersensitive is hyposensitive. When this occurs, the child is under-sensitive, or his brain under-reacts to sensations. He is a sensory seeker, needs additional stimulation, and may want to continuously touch, feel, climb, jump, or spin around. He may crave intense sensations, which might over-stimulate the average child. A hyposensitive child typically has a higher tolerance for pain. For example, he may frequently crash into the sofa. He may require a higher intensity of sensation or activity.

Children with hypersensitivity are sensory avoiders; children who are hyposensitive are sensory seekers. Both have atypical responses to sensations. A child may also experience a combination of both sensations.

SPEECH PROBLEMS

By age two a child should be saying between 50 and 100 words. On his second birthday Roman could not say *anything!* He was an entire year behind in language. "Children with tactile defensiveness often have problems learning to talk because they do no receive adequate information from the touch receptors in and around the face and mouth,"[10] according to Trott. As a result, it was a difficult challenge getting Roman to speak. Roman had excellent receptive language. This is the ability to comprehend other people's spoken language and the use of facial expressions, gestures, and nonverbal language. But Roman had no expressive language or individual words. Expressive language is the ability to communicate your thoughts and feelings to others using a common language (spoken, written, or sign).

SPEECH TECHNIQUES

Roman had speech therapy once a week for an hour, but this wasn't adequate intervention time for teaching him how to talk. He had an excellent speech therapist who taught me various techniques to encourage talking.

Many techniques were not working, though, so the speech therapist was contemplating teaching him sign language. I didn't want him to learn to sign because I wanted him to talk. I needed him to start saying words soon so we wouldn't have to begin sign language, so I thought of a different approach.

I began my own individual speech class with him for at least an hour everyday. I showed him different toys and taught him to say the name of them. When I read to him, I always pointed to different pictures in the story and encouraged him to pronounce the word associated with that picture. I continued speech lessons throughout the day during all his skills, drills, and playtime.

I figured that since he couldn't say a complete word maybe he could pronounce individual letters; these are called graphemes. I wanted these sounds to be meaningful and beneficial, so I decided to encourage him to talk by teaching him the alphabet. Roman had excellent memory skills and was able to learn one letter a day. I began with the letter "A." As we went along, he could say some of the individual letter sounds and that encouraged me. If he couldn't say a letter, I would have him point to it.

Eventually this method worked and he began to pronounce various letters. I cheered if he could say a letter and that motivated him to keep trying. Even though he couldn't say all the letters, he knew the whole alphabet in 26 days. That was a huge accomplishment and it taught me more about his cognitive capabilities and his ability to learn and retain information quickly. Cognitive development is the process used for the tasks of remembering, reasoning, understanding, and using judgment. Every day we went over the letters until he could say almost all of them. I knew that if he could say the letters then he could eventually say words. (I just had to keep prying them out of him.)

After he learned all the letters, I decided to do numbers. They were all single syllabic sounds. I began with one and worked my way up to ten. Again, if he couldn't say the number, I had him point to it. And just as with the letters, he learned one number a day. At two years and two months he knew the entire alphabet and the numbers one to ten and could pronounce most of them. With his speech therapist working with him and showing me ways to position his lips and tongue when trying to say a word, I knew we were on a roll.

WORDS, WORDS, AND MORE WORDS

I knew if he could say "B," he would eventually say single syllabic words. I gave him a ball and told him to say "ball." And one day he finally said "ball!" I was so excited. I told him to say "ball" again. And he said it. I hugged him and he laughed. "Can you say it again?" I asked.

"Ball," he laughed. He was learning how to say words on command. This was huge.

As he began learning a few words, I wrote them down and began a word chart. Each day I had him repeat the words he had said previously so he wouldn't forget how to say them, and then I encouraged him to say more words. Then it finally clicked; each day he began picking up more words. My word list was getting longer and each day he would repeat all the words. By the time he was two and a half, he had about 90 words. I could not believe it! Now that he was learning how to say words, I advanced him to saying sentences. I began with three, four, and easy five-word sentences using many of the words he knew how to say. I gave him a simple sentence to repeat, for example, "I want a cookie," or "Go to park." I would not allow him to express or ask for something without putting it into a sentence.

Another activity that tremendously increased his language abilities was the reading exercises we did each night before he went to bed. I read between two and four books and made up simple sentences about the different pictures in the books for him to repeat, for example, "This is a dog," "The boy is on the bike," "The tree is tall." This not only increased his language but also his attention span. I told him what to say and made him repeat it. Over time he went from four-word sentences to eight-word sentences, such as, "He likes to go swimming in the park." I actually counted the number of words he said when he said something. I did these reading language drills for one year, and by the end of that year Roman was completely age appropriate for speech and language.

The next skill we worked on was speech articulation – teaching him how to pronounce each word clearly. I gave him a sentence, and if he couldn't clearly pronounce the word, I showed him how to say it correctly. For example, he would say, "The gass is geen." I taught him how to growl by saying "Grrrr." He repeated "Grrr." "Now say grrrreen." Then he could say green and grass.

Once he was age appropriate in speech and sentence structure, we worked on language pragmatics – correct usage of pronouns, proper manners, and diction. I taught him proper social skills and what to say when you meet and greet someone, for example, "I'm glad to meet you," "Nice to see you again," "Have a great day." We practiced how to look people in the eye and have a firm handshake when meeting and having conversation with someone. We worked on conversational speech and how to respond to questions such as, "How are you doing today?" "I am doing great," "What is your favorite sport?" "I like to play soccer." Practicing social skills improved his language and increased his confidence and ability to appropriately converse with others.

Chapter Eight

Foes and Friends

nother aspect of the skills and drills program was going to the library once a week. Having access to a good library is extremely beneficial and important. When Roman was two, his ECI service coordinator, Melanie, recommended that I take him to the library for reading time. Once a week the librarian read stories to the children, and what should have been a pleasant and welcoming occasion was very embarrassing and stressful for me. Roman was the only child who wouldn't sit still for the story.

All the other children (age two to four) could sit and listen, but Roman wanted to stand up and run around. I told Melanie that he wasn't ready for this yet because he could not sit still. I wanted to try again in about six months, but she explained how important it was that he learned how to sit appropriately in a social environment. I didn't mind having to reprimand him at home when he wouldn't sit, but doing so in public was sheer humiliation for me.

He began to fuss if I tried to force him to sit. The librarian understood, but some of the parents would stare at him, and then at me. They thought he was just ill-mannered. (After all, their kids were perfect, attentive, and never did anything wrong.) Each week I made him try to sit, and when he wouldn't, I had a special time-out place in the library for him.

I remember one lady in particular, who I'll refer to as "Heartless." She was quick to express her displeasure in him by pulling her son away and not allowing him to go near my son. (I guess she figured he might catch what Roman had.) Her son wanted to play with Roman, but she would not let him. I was extremely offended and thought, "That's okay. One day, lady, I'll show you." I said, "C'mon Roman, we have a lot of work to do." It was people like her that made me more determined to get him well.

Month after month I took Roman to the library for reading time. Month after month I would have to put him in time-out, and month after month I had to endure Heartless's offensive stares. Melanie saw how rude she was and told me to ignore her. She continued to encourage me not to give up because Roman could do this. She had such incredible faith in him.

Since sitting still was such a struggle for him, I decided to practice "library reading" at home. I put a mat on the floor and had him sit in front of me. I read from a chair just like the librarian did. I set a timer and told him that he was not to get up until the timer went off. At first he only sat for one minute, then three minutes, and then we increased to five minutes. Over the next few weeks he began sitting for ten minutes, and within a few months he could sit for 30 minutes and actually loved reading time!

Most people were very kind and endearing, but I had to learn how to handle the few who were rude and learn not to be ashamed. Roman is who he is, and I had to overcome my embarrassment when he misbehaved. No child is perfect, and some are going to have disabilities. As mothers and as a society we must love, embrace, and accept that this is how the child is and not feel ashamed or feel like a failure as a mother.

Accept his goodness, his victories, and his determination to get better, even if he can't. Let your tears be for his endeavors, not for his failures, for this may be what God has for you. There is one prayer I often prayed: "Lord, if it is your will for me to have a child with autism, please show me how to live with it." In that moment of prayer, I realized that acceptance was my only option. I did not want to become bitter or covetous of other moms who had "normal" children.

You've Got a Friend

It was not that difficult sharing my son's diagnosis with my friends because I was constantly complaining about the fact that Roman had difficulty eating or talking. They had never heard of Sensory Processing Disorder and, like me, didn't understand the full ramifications of the diagnosis. On the other hand, I was embarrassed to tell them about the autism symptoms because I was afraid of the stigma that is attached to autism. When I explained that there was a possibility of him being autistic, they were stunned and at a loss for words. Most mothers who are not exposed to this world do not fully understand what autism represents. I explained to them that I was fighting for my child's life. When I first told them, I was worried that they may not want their children around Roman, but that was not the case. Fortunately, they were empathetic and many reached out to offer their help.

We continued our weekly play dates, and because he was still so young, many of his behaviors didn't bother my friends. They were never condescending or judgmental. I knew that they were concerned for me and my son and probably thought, "What if this was my child? What would I do? How would I feel?"

Sometimes it was difficult for them to understand why I had to completely restructure my life and could not go with them to the movies, restaurants, or social gatherings anymore. I told them that I had to maintain a strict schedule and had to get to bed early in order to continue my rigorous program. They often inquired why I had to do many of the things I was doing, but I always remained positive and prayerful. Although I was able to maintain most of my friendships during those three years, because of time constraints I spent very little time with my friends. It is nearly impossible to sustain your friendships as they once were when you have a child with autism. I don't think anyone can fully realize your burden unless they have to deal with it themselves.

The only problem I had with my friends was my own feelings about my child's inadequacy, my own selfish pride about how this reflected on me and what I wanted for our son. I sometimes became frustrated and jealous and thought, "Why did this happen to our son? What if he never overcomes all the problems that beset him? He will never be able to function appropriately in society." I had to constantly pray away my feelings of covetousness and sorrow and stay focused on the goal that was set before me – Roman's recovery. I didn't have time to lament and say, "Woe is me." And when I did go to that place, I allowed myself to grieve and then got back to the task at hand.

CHAPTER NINE

Eat and Sleep

Roman had a difficult time eating because he had problems with oral motor skills and something called oral defensiveness. Children can have tactile defensive sensations in the mouth. They may have an aversion to certain food textures or tastes or have difficulty with fine motor muscle movements in the mouth and tongue.

Roman couldn't tolerate the textures and tastes of most foods. He could barely chew and swallow and didn't like to put anything in or around his mouth. Even as late as 16 months, he would choke on simple foods like mashed potatoes and macaroni. I used to actually tremble when it was time to feed him because he could barely eat anything and refused to try most new foods. He was very hungry, but he couldn't eat. He couldn't blow out a candle or drink from a straw and wouldn't even lick a lollipop. He wouldn't let a toy microphone touch his mouth and wouldn't blow through a toy instrument, such as a flute or harmonica.

When Roman began speech therapy, his therapist taught me how to do face and mouth massages to stimulate his mouth. This helped alleviate his defensiveness. I laid him down on the bed and for five minutes I massaged his whole face. Then, using a finger guard, I massaged inside his mouth, including his tongue, inside his cheeks, his gums, and the roof of his mouth. He liked this stimulation and it felt good to him. I did this twice a day for three months.

The mouth massages helped him overcome all of his oral defensiveness and his chewing and swallowing problems, and he was eventually able to blow out a candle, sip from a straw, blow bubbles, and put toys in his mouth. The massages relaxed and stimulated his mouth, and I believe this also assisted with his language skills and ability to formulate words. The massages also desensitized his mouth, allowing him to be more tolerant of foods. Roman was beginning to at least try more foods and could tolerate more textures. He was learning how to chew and swallow without choking. He eventually had a small repertoire of healthy meals that he actually liked to eat. The occupational therapist also taught Roman how to chew gum because chewing gum strengthens oral motor skills, and provides a calm sensation, organization, and proprioceptive input to the mouth, tongue, cheeks, and jaws.

GLUTEN FREE/CASEIN FREE

Many children with autism have trouble eating because of gastrointestinal (GI) tract and digestive problems, such as diarrhea, constipation, and esophagitis. These problems may intensify the autistic symptoms and require medical intervention. Some are placed on a Gluten-Free, Casein-Free diet (GFCF). Gluten is a protein found in wheat, rye, barley, and oats, and casein is a protein found in dairy.

The removal of these foods from their diets has been known to help alleviate repetitive habits, regulate bowl movements, and improve the child's behavior. According to the Sante Rehabilitation Group, "Some doctors and therapists believe that it helps decrease unwanted behaviors (not paying attention, poor socialization, speech delays, repetitive actions) and increase desired developmental skills and appropriate behaviors (paying attention, age appropriate, socialization, increased language)."[11]

The negative aspects of the diet are the expense, availability, and preparation of the food. Roman's nutritionist was contemplating putting Roman on the GFCF diet, but she determined his feeding problems were sensory related, not caused by digestive trouble. Parents must work with a dietician or physician to determine if healthy GFCF or other diet or medical intervention is necessary.

Got Milk?

I planned on nursing for one full year because I knew of all the health benefits of breast milk. For the first two weeks, I was able to substitute the bottle along with the nursing, but once Roman became used to breast milk, he would no longer take a bottle again, *ever*. He didn't like the feel of the nipple on any bottle, nor would he ever take a pacifier. I didn't know anything about oral defensiveness then, but I now understand that even as a newborn he was orally defensive.

Because Roman couldn't tolerate most foods, he would fill himself up by nursing. Needless to say, when he turned one year old, there wasn't any way I could stop him from nursing because it was still his main source of nutrition. Although it was a sacrifice to nurse this long, baby formula costs about $1,400 for the first year. What I lost in freedom, I saved in my pocket.

The not-so-good news was that Roman was always tall for his age. As he approached 18 months, it didn't look right to everyone else for such an older baby to still be nursing. Everyone always thought he was at least a year or two older than he was. I remember getting lots of grief from well-meaning family and friends about the fact that I was nursing too long. No one understood that it wasn't just that he wanted to continue nursing; nursing was also a source of comfort to his restless spirit. As more autism symptoms began to manifest, Roman's frustration grew and nursing was his way of calming down. When he cried and became frustrated, nursing consoled him. However, I knew that I had to eventually wean him from breast milk, and this, too, was yet another struggle.

There was a tremendous benefit to nursing this long. My doctor knew that this was going to be our only child, so she advised me to continue nursing him until he turned two. Most women are aware of what the health benefits of nursing are for a baby; they not aware of what the health advantages are for the mother.

My doctor explained that if a woman nurses for two complete years, whether consecutively or with different children, she could reduce her chances for developing breast cancer by 50%. That was of great significance to me because my grandmother died of breast cancer when she was only 39, making my risks for developing this disease much greater. This was a great excuse and allowed me more time for weaning. I can laugh now because he actually did me a huge favor by wanting to nurse for so long. While I was helping him, he was inadvertently helping me.

Right before Roman turned two, I began telling him that he was going to have to stop nursing, and he began to protest. I slowly transitioned him from breast to the sippy-cup. I had to do my proverbial countdowns and tell him just two minutes, then one minute, 10 seconds, etc. In the beginning he cried, but after a few months he reluctantly accepted the fact that he had to stop nursing, and I was finally able to wean him.

SUGARPLUM THOUGHTS AND LOLLIPOP DREAMS

Thankfully, Roman slept 12 hours every night. The autism never affected his ability to get a good night's sleep. This may be due to the fact that from infancy I always had a consistent and serene bedtime routine, making sure he was asleep by 7:30. When Roman was two, he went through a short period of having irrational fears about nothing when it was time for him to go to sleep. These "bedtime fears," as I called them, reduced him to tears. I couldn't understand what caused this because there wasn't any frightening or negative incident that had occurred in his life that might have triggered this change. Just like with all his other bad habits, I had to figure out how to combat this so it wouldn't become a nightly ritual.

When he began to fret about the inane things that he conjured up in his mind, I immediately stopped and redirected him to think happy thoughts. I would say, "No bedtime fears and tears; only happy thoughts." Then I listed many wonderful, happy things in his life to think about.

Being an ardent lover of musicals, I made up a song to the tune of "Happy Talk" from the musical *South Pacific*, and it goes as follows:

> Think of happy thoughts, happy thoughts;
> Think about things you like to do.
> You have to think happy, and you will be happy,
> And happy thoughts will come to you.
>
> Think about a boy, playing with his toys;
> These are all the things that he enjoys:
> His cars and his planes, his wagon, and his trains;
> These are all the thoughts he entertains.
>
> Think of happy thoughts, happy thoughts;
> Think about things you like to do.
> If you just think happy, then you will be happy,
> And happy thoughts will stay with you.

Invariably, when I sang that song to him each night, he changed his focus to happy thoughts. I always finished the song by saying, "Have sugarplum thoughts and lollipop dreams" (meaning have sweet thoughts and dreams). Then he smiled and soon slipped off into a peaceful night's sleep.

I share this particular story because we, as mothers, have to have the ability to come up with our own creative techniques to fight the pernicious behaviors that can overtake our child. The more you practice helping your child, the more the innovative ideas will come to you.

CHAPTER TEN

Gross and Fine Motor Problems

nother issue I had to deal with involved problems with gross motor control. Gross motor activities involve large muscle movements in the arms, legs, and trunk, necessary for things like running, jumping, and climbing. Roman's gross motor problems stemmed from the fact that he had a difficult problem with gravity, which made him fearful of having his feet off the ground. He had gravitational insecurity, a form of over-responsiveness to vestibular sensations.

> According to Jane Case-Smith, "The vestibular system is the sense of movement and gravity. It is through the vestibular system that we develop a relationship with the earth, that is, knowing what side is up, upside down, left, right, horizontal, and vertical. Vestibular input tells us whether or not we are moving, how quickly and what direction we are moving. It provides us with the sense and safety that come only from knowing that one's feet are planted firmly on the ground."[12]

Roman did not want his feet to leave the ground while playing, thus making him afraid of many non-threatening, fun activities that children normally engage in. As a result, he was afraid to jump or hop, go on a seesaw, swing from a monkey bar, go on a tire swing, or even jump from the bottom stair of the stairway in our home.

I purchased a mini-trampoline to help him learn to jump. Roman was apprehensive in the beginning and, at first, I had to hold him while I jumped with him in my arms. To lessen his anxiety, I sang songs and played music while we jumped. Over time I placed him on the trampoline and he was able to jump by himself. Jumping gives input to the vestibular system. This is also beneficial because after they bounce they are able to focus better on paper/pencil tasks because bouncing is a self-calming activity for some children.

Children who have a fear of jumping have an insecure relationship to gravity characterized by excessive fear during ordinary movement activities. The gravitationally insecure child is overwhelmed by changes in head position and movement, especially when moving backward or upward through space. Fear of heights, even those involving only slight distances from the ground, is a common problem associated with this condition. Jane Case-Smith continues to say,

> "Children who display gravitational insecurity often show signs of 'atypical' fear, anxiety, or avoidance in relation to stairs, escalators or elevators, moving or high pieces of playground equipment, and uneven or unpredictable surfaces. Some children are so insecure that only a small change from one surface to another, as when stepping off the curb or from the sidewalk to the grass, is enough to send them into a state of high anxiety or panic."[13]

PARK THERAPY

To help with his gross motor problems and gravitational insecurities, we went to the playground every afternoon for "park therapy." Playgrounds have a multitude of beneficial opportunities for movement. An activity such as going backward and forward on a swing is great for the vestibular system. I had Roman do a variety of playground activities to help him get his feet off the ground. He had to slide, run, go on the seesaw, hang from the monkey bars, and jump on and off different equipment. I held his hand or helped him balance on most of the playground equipment until he felt safe.

There were a few activities, as simple as crawling through a tunnel, which Roman was fearful of and I tried different techniques to help him overcome his fears with playground equipment. Because Roman had visual perceptual problems, he did not want to crawl through a tunnel or slide down a covered slide because he could not see the end, did not know what was on the other side, and was uncertain of what would happen. Roman was afraid of the unknown.

I didn't know exactly what his fears were, but I knew I had to make him feel safe in order to get him through this. I began by standing at the other end of the tunnel and encouraging him to crawl through, but he would only shake his head "No." Next, I repeatedly crawled through the tunnel myself and told him how fun it was, but he still would not budge. I tried everything I could think of but nothing seemed to work. I needed a new strategy.

Since Roman's favorite candy was MandM's, I brought a small bag of them to the park and placed them in the middle of the tunnel. He wanted the candy, but he would have to crawl through the tunnel to get it. When he fussed I said, "Roman, if you want the candy, then crawl through the tunnel and get it." He absolutely didn't want to do it.

So I crawled through from the other end and sat in the middle of the tunnel. I ate one of the MandM's and said, "Mmmm, yummy." He frowned and started to crawl in (he didn't want me eating his candy), but then crawled out again. As I ate another one, he fussed and tried crawling in again. He got a little farther along, then looked up, realized where he was, got scared, and stopped.

"C'mon, you can do it," I said, smiling. "You're almost to the MandM's. Hooray!" (It is extremely important that you give lots of praise and encouragement when they are trying to accomplish these small tasks, because in their minds they truly feel threatened.) He continued a little farther, and then started to turn around. I said, "I guess I'll have to eat all the MandM's by myself. Mm-Mmm, they sure do taste good." Then he turned back around and kept crawling towards me while I cheered him on. He finally got to the MandM's and ate them.

"You did it!" I exclaimed, but I didn't want to startle him too much because he was still apprehensive. I then told him to follow me while I crawled out so he would have to crawl all the way through the tunnel, and he did. I immediately had him follow me through the tunnel again. I said, "See how much fun the tunnel is?" Roman began to smile as he became more self-assured and realized that the other end was safe. After following me through a few times, he crawled through it by himself. I stood at the other end so he could see me and he was able to crawl through the tunnel with ease. From that point on, he had no more tunnel fears. This is just an example of one of the many strategies you can come up with to help a child overcome his fears.

FINE MOTOR PROBLEMS

Roman also had fine motor control problems involving the specific use of small muscles in the fingers, hands, toes, mouth, tongue, and lips. A child with autism may also have poor eye-hand coordination. Again Maryann Colby Trott states, "Children whose tactile system is dysfunctional are likely to have a difficult time learning fine motor skills because it is through the discriminative system that the brain receives the feedback necessary to develop feeding, dressing, writing, and other fine motor skills."[14]

Roman could not hold a spoon or crayon correctly, he had trouble bringing his cup or spoon to his mouth to drink or eat, and I had to feed him until he was two and one half years old. Roman had poor oral motor control of his mouth muscles for sucking, swallowing, chewing, and speaking. His fine motor problems were a result of dyspraxia, defined as difficulty planning and carrying out motor actions, but dyspraxia can involve either fine or gross motor control problems.

Praxis is what allows us to efficiently plan, organize, and execute all kinds of skills, and is critical to sensory processing development. Motor planning is the ability to organize and sequence tasks in a coordinated manner. It allows a child to combine and use various motor skills to execute more intricate acts. These skills are necessary for functioning successfully in one's everyday physical environment. For example, a child could have trouble holding food steady on a spoon and bringing it up to the mouth without spilling. He also may struggle with learning how to talk, chew, swallow, button, tie a shoe, or cut with scissors. These are all motor planning problems.

PROPRIOCEPTION: DEEP PRESSURE AND JOINT COMPRESSION

Roman also experienced a problem with proprioception, which is understanding where your body is in space. (For example, knowing whether you are standing or sitting.) It can be a problem if you perceive sensations atypically. Children who experience difficulty with proprioception may appear clumsy, awkward, or distracted. They may have difficulty regulating the force they apply to an activity (writing or clapping) or with the limits of personal space. They seek certain behaviors in order to figure out where their bodies are in space.

Roman responded to a friendly touch, such as a hug, as though it were offensive or frightening. It was obvious and insulting to people when he lashed out or backed away from their greetings, so his occupational therapist taught me how to do "brushing." Using a soft, surgical hospital brush, I brushed his arms, legs, hands, back, and feet, ten times each, followed by ten compressions of each major joint (shoulder, elbow, wrist, hip, knee, and ankle). I first had to massage his whole body, including his face, arms, legs, back, hands, feet, every finger, and every toe.

These techniques helped reduce his hypersensitivity, hyperactivity, anxiety, and stimming, and helped him feel relaxed and calm. The brushing and joint compressions are used to help organize

77

the sensory system. Deep body pressure and joint compression organize and calm the tactile and proprioceptive systems. The massage helped his brain regulate the sensations that came in. This was absolutely essential in order for him to tolerate and overcome his fear of touching things and allowing others to touch him.

After six months of the massage procedures, Roman no longer had proprioception difficulties with people touching him. He began to love giving hugs and being hugged by others. It was truly remarkable! I never had to give him another massage after six months. You take your health for granted until you have a child with a disability that makes him afraid of a simple thing like a hug.

Roman's proprioception dysfunction also affected his desire to put things on his head and face; he also didn't like anything over or in his ears. He wouldn't even allow the telephone to touch his ears. One of the stations I had was called "Costumes/Dress-up." This was great for proprioception development, oral motor skills, and imaginative play. I purchased a variety of boy's Halloween costumes for him to put on and play with so he could get used to putting things on his face and head. I had "Bob the Builder," fireman, policeman, and "Thomas the Engine Train" costumes. Each costume provided him with assorted opportunities to place things over his face and head that he would not have otherwise wanted to put on.

Roman loved to build with blocks and he built something everyday. I told him that he should dress like a builder so he could be a "real builder." In spite of his great reluctance, I was able to convince him to put on a construction hat and goggles. He still didn't like anything on his head, but I told him that in order to be a "real builder" he had to wear them. He was finally able to put them on and over time was able to tolerate the feeling of various things on his head and face. I soon began having him act in our own pretend theatrical plays, wearing other costumes that had components for his head and face. This imaginative play was great for language development, and the costumes helped desensitize him to touch on his face and head – he was no longer afraid to wear hats, masks, or eye wear.

CHAPTER ELEVEN

Transitions

Right around two years of age Roman began having difficulty with transitions – going from one place or one activity to another. After completing an activity, I could no longer say "All done, let's clean up" without him having a complete meltdown. I had to give him a warning that an activity was about to end. I began to have actual transitions before leaving any place, like the store, park, or church. I had to have countdowns before ending one skill and beginning another. I would say, "You have five more minutes, two more minutes, one minute, 20 seconds." Then I counted from one to ten before he could calmly end an activity. Ending something abruptly only upset him and he would react inappropriately. Roman also needed to have transitions at home for skills and drills, or when it was time to take a bath, eat meals, or even turn off the television.

There was a period of time when he had meltdowns at the park when I told him it was time to leave. He cried, screamed, and fell to the ground, and I literally dragged him out of the park with every mom staring at me. It was sheer humiliation for me. I knew it was important to go to the park, but I also knew I had to get him out of this new tantrum phase, so I began warning him before we got there that he was not to cry when I told him it was time to leave. I told Roman I would give him a countdown and he was to come. But for some strange reason, when the time came to go home, he would still lose control. This went on for a few months. I did the countdowns, but it remained a battle.

One afternoon at the park I finally reached my breaking point. I admonished, "Ten more minutes until we leave, and no crying!"

He said, "Okay, Mommy."

Then I said, "Five more minutes."

"Yes, Mommy."

Again I warned, "Two more minutes." He then came off the swing and ran over to and climbed to the top of the biggest slide in the park.

I said to myself, "This kid is slick. He is actually climbing to the top of that slide so I won't be able get to him." I could feel my temperature rise. I quickly walked over and yelled up to him, "One more minute!"

Roman became frantic. "No, Mommy, not yet!"

Now I was really getting mad. I gritted my teeth and said, "Thirty more seconds, Roman, and I mean it!"

He cried, "No, Mommy!"

Then I counted from one to ten and said emphatically, "Come down here right now!" He refused.

All the kids there stood as still as statues, watching the drama of Mama and son at the park. I angrily climbed up the steep slide towards him, and he ran the other way down the stairs. The kids began to laugh. I went down the stairs and made chase after him. Guess where he went next? Remember that tunnel that he used to be afraid to go into? He ran and sat right in the middle where he thought I couldn't reach him. I frantically crawled in after him, only for him to flee out the other side. I was livid!

When I caught him, I dragged him out of the park kicking and screaming with the whispers of the parents and the laughter of the children slowly fading behind me. That was it! I told him, "No more park until you stop that crying." I warned him that he better not ever run away from me again, and that I was not going to tolerate his unacceptable behavior.

We didn't go to the park for the next three days. Roman kept asking to go, but I told him no because he was on punishment. He cried and we did his time-out routine for three days, but the next time we went to the park, guess what? When I gave him the countdown to leave, he left without incident. He wanted to tantrum, but he didn't dare. The next couple of days were tenuous, but he remembered the consequence and quietly left. We never had another tantrum at the park after that.

After about a year of doing countdowns, all of the transitioning issues disappeared and he overcame his anxiety around having to leave or finish one thing and begin something else. The repetition of the countdowns allowed his brain to process that something was about to end. Roman's mind became settled and confident that everything was going to be fine even when whatever task he was doing was over. I never had to do countdowns again and no longer had any transition problems.

Just like the tantrums in the park, some undesirable behaviors just come out of nowhere. We would conquer one problem, and a new one would develop. But each new issue had to be immediately and properly addressed and corrected. I didn't want to have to take on another issue, but each new dilemma had to be rectified. Otherwise the problem would only intensify and escalate.

BEHAVIORAL INTERVENTION/PREP TIME

By the time Roman was two and a half, many of the skills and drills techniques were working and he had overcome many of his autistic and sensory problems. Unfortunately, he began developing more behavioral problems. He became increasingly obstinate and confrontational when told to do something. Roman, like any two-year-old, could be challenging, but the "terrible two's" were much more pronounced with autism. Like all the other issues he had to overcome, developing proper behavioral skills was also mandatory.

Melanie suggested that I put Roman into a preschool program to help him overcome some of his behavioral problems and separation anxiety. She said it would also be beneficial to Roman because he would be around other children his age and would imitate their appropriate play and behavior. But before I could do that, I knew I had more work to do with him on his behavior. Otherwise, when he turned three he might have to enter a behavioral intervention classroom. I knew that would be detrimental for him because Roman was an imitator and would probably pick up the other children's inappropriate behaviors. So, over the next three months, I implemented my own behavioral intervention program at home. I repeatedly sent him to time-out in order to get him to follow directions. He had to learn to stop complaining and do what he was told.

Part of my behavioral intervention to prepare Roman for preschool I called "preschool prep time." I targeted an area he needed to change, modeled the behavior that I wanted him to display, and had him imitate me. Modeling is one of the most efficient ways to teach children appropriate behaviors.

We role-played what was going to happen at school and what to expect. I read books to Roman about preschool and told him what he was going to be doing. He had to listen, behave, and follow my directions. I had him sit at his desk and taught him to raise his hands if he wanted something. I taught him how to walk quietly in line behind me, proper manners such as saying "Please," "Thank you," and "Yes, Ma'am" to his teacher, and how to properly conduct himself in a school setting.

If Roman fussed or complained, he went right to time-out where he was strictly warned that he was expected to behave. For three months I ran his drills and skills like a preschool; I acted like a teacher and he the student. As a result, by the time Roman began his preschool program, he was much more prepared.

A month before Roman was to begin, I took him to the school and showed him around. I took pictures of the school, his teachers, his classroom, gym, and library. I then pasted them onto paper and made a book. I wrote a short story about his school and what he would be doing and how much fun it was going to be. I read this to him everyday for a few weeks, and he became excited and was looking forward to starting.

It is so important that you always have prep time before your child begins something new or goes anywhere new so he will be less intimidated. Get a book and read to him about places that he may be going, such as the doctor, dentist, zoo, birthday parties, library, and restaurants. This will allow the child to be prepared and he will understand what he will be doing and how he is to behave.

READY–SET–PRESCHOOL

When Roman finally learned to stop being so combative, he was able to focus and complete all the different tasks. Just before he turned three, he began a "Mother's Day Out" church preschool program and went twice a week from 9:00 until 2:00. I first met with his teachers and told them about his disability and explained to them how to deal with his issue of transitions, along with certain fears and touch issues. Like most teachers, they had never heard of Sensory Processing Disorder, but they were eager to learn and use the techniques I showed them and were very understanding and sensitive to his needs. It is extremely important that you tell any preschool teacher, or day-care or home-care worker, about all of the problems your child may have and how you deal with them. This will allow your child to have success in the classroom and will enable the teacher to properly address the issues and needs of the student.

I eased Roman into the preschool by first allowing him to go just two hours and eventually built up to the full day over the next month. Because of all the preschool prep time we did, he actually did extremely well. Roman never cried. He enjoyed the structure of being in the classroom and loved doing all the activities.

The ECI service coordinator, Melanie, went to his classroom one hour a week to observe how he was doing and to intervene if the teachers needed assistance. As a result of all the skills and drills, along with the preschool prep time, he didn't require any help in preschool. Roman was compliant, followed directions, could sit for long periods of time, and accomplished all of the assigned tasks and projects. With all the arts and crafts we had done in skills and drills, he was adept at using all of the fun supplies they had in preschool.

He was confident and secure, imitated and played well with the other children, and developed appropriate social skills. (This is very important because most children with autism have a very difficult time socially.) Surprisingly, he even wanted to try some different foods he saw the other kids eating in their lunches. Roman thrived in the classroom because he was trained in a structured environment. The skills and drills program made it possible for him to do well in school right from the start. We still weren't out of the woods yet, though, because we still had many autistic, fine and gross motor, and behavioral issues to work on at home. But his success in the classroom was an encouraging development.

Chapter Twelve

The Abyss

By the time Roman was three, he had overcome many of his autistic behaviors, and I was proud of the fact that we were well on our way to conquering the autism. He was doing so well that we made plans to visit my family and spend a couple of weeks at camp again that summer. Then the most frightening day of my life occurred.

One cold February evening I told Roman he had to get ready for bed. It was only 6:15, but I was going to begin his nighttime routine. For the first time, he looked at me in a frightful way and began to tantrum. But this was no ordinary tantrum; he began to scream and rage. My mother was down visiting and we froze in horror because we had never seen him behave like this before.

I kept saying, "Roman, calm down! What's wrong with you?" He began running in circles, screaming, and then began running up and down the stairs. When I tried to stop him, he punched and kicked at me. He kept crying and yelling, "No, no, no, stay away from me!" Then he ran into a closet, closed the door, and wailed. When I tried to get him out he began raging at me again – screaming, kicking, and finally throwing himself on the floor in anguish.

I tried to pick him up, but he took off again, running and crying.

By then my mother and I were crying also. She said, "What is wrong with him? Stop him from doing that!"

"I'm trying!" I yelled. "I don't know what's happening to him!" We were truly horrified.

He continued running and screaming and wouldn't let me get near him. This was the first time ever that I couldn't touch him. The most frightening thing was the way he looked; it appeared as if he didn't know me. "It's me, Roman, your mother. Let me hold you," I pleaded.

He kept shaking his head, "No, no, stay away!" Then he bellowed out in such fury that I thought he was in extreme pain. He wailed as he ran furiously up and down the stairs, in and out of the closet, into different rooms of our house. For the life of me I could not stop him. I finally tried to restrain him and he bit and scratched like a wild animal; he was violent and uncontrollable, and was I unable to console him.

Suddenly the yelling stopped and he sat in silence, staring into what I refer to as "the abyss." He did not know where he was, and I did not know what to do. I was so frightened that at that very moment I envisioned myself falling into my own dark whole… trembling. I did not want to move. "Just be still," I said to myself, "Then you won't have to think…work…do….but one of us has to do something…me first."

I went over to him and gently whispered, "Roman, are you okay?" But he didn't see me; he looked right through me. I couldn't reach him. I repeatedly waved my hand in front of his face and called his name, but his eyes didn't flinch. He only had a blank stare. When I finally tried to hold him, he began a piercing shrill, a sound that paralyzed my senses. All the natural sounds were silenced.

I found myself caught in a trap of time. I was too petrified to move, but Roman could. He proceeded to continue his rant, storming through the house. My mother was frantically saying, "Oh my God! This can't be happening! He's not even there! He doesn't even seem to know who you are! " By now we are both beside ourselves in absolute terror.

My mother's first thought was to take him to the emergency room, but that would involve having him sedated. I had never used drugs on him and wasn't going to start now. Then she had the good sense to tell me to call his psychologist. Fortunately I was able to get her on the phone. She could hear him hollering in the background and asked, "Elizabeth, is that Roman screaming? What's wrong?"

I anxiously said, "I'm losing him! I've never seen this before! I can't calm him down! I can't get to him. He doesn't even know who I am, and he's not coming out of it! What should I do? Please help me!" She calmly told me to pick him up and put him in the car and drive him around. I told her he wouldn't let me near him. She said to just grab him and put him in his car seat, turn on the classical music he loves to listen to, and drive around.

I was afraid to go near him, but I picked him up and forcefully placed him in the car. My mom took the phone and was in tears while talking to the psychologist. I could hear her explaining what had happened while I frantically drove off. He continued to scream and cry and I turned up the music. I drove around our city in tears for what seemed like an eternity, but in reality was only about 15 minutes, and then he suddenly began to calm down. His cries turned to whimpers. I continued looking back at him, trying to appease him by saying, "Hear the beautiful music, Roman? I just love this song."

Eventually, as quickly as it had begun, the ordeal ended. He looked at me calmly and said, "Oh, hello, Mommy. Where are we going?" I almost ran off the road. He knew who I was again. I pulled over and stopped the car, ran to the back seat, hugged him, and told him how much I loved him. He had no idea what had happened. No recollection at all. I asked him how he was feeling and he said that he felt fine.

I was afraid to go back home because I didn't know if he would start to scream again. *What triggers this?* I thought. As we drove into the garage, my mother was watching for me and I mouthed to her that he was okay. Roman greeted her happily, saying, "Hello, Grandmama!" She was relieved to see that he was back to normal. I whispered to her what had happened, then took him upstairs and quietly rocked him to sleep.

Although we had been able to calm him, I was trembling over what had taken place that night. Mother said, "I have been through a lot and have seen many things, but I have never been that terrified in my entire life." Fear became redefined at that moment for both of us. She said, "What is happening to him? I have never seen any child slip away like that! You're in trouble, Elizabeth."

Never before had words rang so true. I knew I was in trouble. I knew that we were in trouble. It's impossible to comprehend or imagine how disassociated from a parent a child with autism can become. I'm so thankful she was there because it was so emotional and frightening that two minds were needed just to sort out the correct course of action to take. But even in our trials, God is wonderful. Not only had he placed me there to support my son, but he placed my mother there as well. It was the circle of life.

That night I fell to my knees in prayer, exhausted, both mentally and physically. I begged the Lord that if He had any love for me at all, to please not take my son from me. I told him I couldn't live if he slipped away. "You said you wouldn't give us more than we can bear, and I just will not be able to bear this. Please, dear God, I beg you to not let me lose him," I prayed.

Fear reappeared the next day. I was neither ready nor willing to relive that experience. No one knows how or why these things occur, but I had gathered enough strength to declare that the abyss was not an option. He was fine the entire day. I remember going to the store with Mother and bursting into tears, saying, "I just can't lose him. We've come so far. He's just about healed!"

My mother tried to console me although all the while she, too, was afraid. She said, "There is no way you can come back to camp this summer. Roman is really in trouble."

I called my brother, Ron Jr., to tell him we would not be coming back to camp and he would have to find someone else to work in our place. When I explained to him what had happened, he, too, was heartbroken. I remember his voice becoming hoarse as he tried to hide his tears and the pain he was feeling. I appreciated his tremendous faith and compassion as he said, "I'm so sorry, Elizabeth, but you must stay strong and not lose hope. Just remember what God has done for him already. You've come so far; you will get through this." My four wonderful, compassionate brothers – each called within the hour offering their condolences, prayers, and words of wisdom to not give up. They all had faith that Roman would get better.

I thought everything would be all right, but the next night, at the exact same time, he began the awful tantrums. He went into the abyss, and again we couldn't reach him. This time I immediately placed him in the car and drove him around while playing the classical music. He calmed down much quicker this time. When he finally came back from wherever he went, he said, "Hello, Mommy. I love you."

Again, I was overcome with grief, and then relief that he came back. When I returned home my mother asked, "What if he does it again and never comes back. What if he slips away forever?" Uncertainty comes with the territory.

On the third night, Tom was home from work. As 6:15 approached, we were terrified that he would begin again. I kept him entertained doing some of the fun activities he liked to do while we both kept watching the clock, our newfound enemy. He continued to play just fine. We were on pins and needles but didn't dare say anything. We stayed outwardly calm and peaceful, making sure he was well entertained. When two hours had passed, I quietly lifted him up and took him to his bedroom. I read him a story and lay down with him until he fell asleep. We finally exhaled with relief when I came downstairs. I felt we had both emerged from a dark whole. Strangely enough, he never had another tantrum, and never went back into the abyss again...*ever.*

I know my prayers were answered. It was as if God gave me a glimpse into what my life could have been. We felt a fear that neither one of us had ever felt before, a fear that brings you to your knees; you do everything within your power not to faint. But my faith sustained me. I had to keep believing. Faith is the substance of things hoped for and evidence of things unseen. All we had was hope, but the end was still not in sight, or so we thought. Oddly enough, from that point on Roman was on his way to a complete healing, and, over the next seven months, we watched all of his bad behaviors simply disappear. By the time he was four, there were no more signs of autistic behavior.

I believe God allowed me to experience that kind of fear so I can relate to what other families with children with autism may have to go through daily and identify with their anguish and despair. To this day, I can't think about that incident without tears coming to my eyes. That's how deeply it affected me. But because of that event, I see the glass half full; I never see it half empty. Everyday the sun is shining for me. I know what could have been, and I'm so grateful for what is.

CHAPTER THIRTEEN

Public School

Early Childhood Intervention services end at age two. Four months before your child's third birthday, your ECI service coordinator will contact the school district and start the transition process, which allows you to meet school personnel and visit the site. After graduating from ECI, your child may receive special education services from your local school district if he is eligible, and/or you can pay for therapies through private agencies. The public school's preschool program will evaluate your child. If he qualifies, you will have an Admission, Review, and Dismissal (ARD) meeting to develop an Individualized Education Plan (IEP), which will determine what services he will receive.

Although Roman had overcome his stimming and touch issues, he still needed speech therapy and some occupational therapy for his fine motor skills. Fortunately for us, he didn't need any behavioral intervention as he had learned how to sit, focus, and attend to all activities. Roman qualified for speech and just a minimal amount of occupational therapy. It wasn't until we met for the ARD when he turned three that he was placed in the category of autistic by the school. The schools do not have a label for Pervasive Developmental Disorder: Not Otherwise Specified (PDD/NOS) or

Sensory Processing Disorder, but under the spectrum of autism, Roman did qualify.

It wasn't until then that I understood that PDD is a non-specific type of autism. This particular autism can affect their speech, behavior, fine and gross motor abilities, and their senses. But strangely enough, it wasn't as difficult hearing it then because he had overcome most of it. I now felt encouraged instead of defeated. I knew that if he could conquer the last of his behavioral quirks and speech problems, there was a chance for full recovery. That was my goal, and we were almost there. When we first began, I had made a checklist of 45 things that were wrong, and I began checking them off as we corrected each problem. After two years of intense therapy I had checked off 41 of them; we only had a few more to go.

Roman's school district offered a wonderful speech class for three- to five-year-olds that were having difficulty learning to talk. On Roman's third birthday he was enrolled in the speech class two days a week for two hours. They also provided an occupational therapist once every six weeks to help him with fine motor skills. The OT provided me with more drills to help Roman with fine motor planning so he could hold a crayon and pencil correctly, cut, button, and zip.

The class was excellent and his teacher had individualized structured lessons to meet each of the student's specific needs. She worked with Roman on pragmatics of language and proper use of pronouns. Whatever he did during class I carried out in his speech skills throughout the day. If he misused a word or had sentence structure problems, I corrected him and taught him to say it the right way. I repeatedly used these methods and eventually he caught on. In just one year not only was he age appropriate in language, his articulation skills were now above his age level. Roman was easily learning sight words, and was beginning to learn to read; I had already taught him all the letter sounds. Since he could sight read, I taught him how to read phonetically. Learning to read was of tremendous benefit for his language development.

We continued all intensive treatment and intervention

throughout the next year. When Roman turned four, he had another Admission, Review, and Dismissal (ARD) because he was being dismissed from the program. He no longer qualified for speech therapy or occupational therapy. He no longer qualified for any services! Roman had officially caught up with speech, was age appropriate for all of his fine motor skills, and could write, draw, button, snap, and zip with ease. The day of victory had come! Roman no longer tested on the autism spectrum!

Chapter Fourteen

Pride and Embarrassment

Once Roman began preschool we could not go to the library for children's hour because it conflicted with school hours. But a year and a half later, when he was four, we went back to visit the library during children's hour. The lady whom I referred to as Heartless was still there sitting so haughtily with her son. I proudly walked in with Roman and the librarian happily greeted us. She hadn't seen us in over a year. Heartless looked over, conspicuously rolled her eyes, and looked away.

Roman sat down and eloquently said, "It's so wonderful to be here again, Ms. Josephine. I really missed reading time." Heartless looked in absolute shock when she heard him speak. She had never heard him say anything before. He sat there calmly, with his hands positioned perfectly in his lap, for the full hour.

As the librarian picked up a final book to read, Roman almost gave Heartless a heart attack when he so politely asked, "Can I read that book to the kids?"

Ms. Josephine, astonished, asked, "Can you read, Roman?"

"I sure can," he replied.

He walked confidently to the front of the room and fluently read the short story to the children. While he read, Heartless sat dumbfounded, clearly astonished by what she was seeing. I'm sure she couldn't understand how this child could change so much in one year. When he finished the story, the children and librarian clapped and said, "Bravo."

Roman quietly sat back down on the floor next to me, put his arm around me, and asked, "Did you like the story I read?" Tears were in my eyes and, without missing a beat, he lovingly whispered, "There are those water drops coming from your eyes again, Mommy." Roman was always descriptive and literal, and I couldn't help but cry.

At the end of the story hour we thanked the librarian and walked past Heartless as she stood there, staring at Roman with her mouth open. Her little boy said hello to Roman, but this time she didn't stop him from trying to engage in conversation. I never acknowledged her, but Roman responded, "Nice to see you again, little boy. Have a great day!" Then we departed the library. Hollywood couldn't have scripted it better.

BE QUIET!

Children with autism can be extremely literal and uninhibited. They often believe things to be exacting, truthful, and accurate; as a result, you have to be much more attentive and protective of their feelings and what they are exposed to. In our child's case, Roman doesn't like anything negative, dishonest, or unkind. Most of the children's shows he watches have to be constructive and positive. Even the G-rated movies and television shows that typical children can watch, Roman gets saddened by.

For example, he didn't want to watch *Rudolf the Red-Nosed Reindeer* because Rudolf's father didn't defend him when the other reindeer teased him about his red nose. Roman couldn't enjoy the movie because he couldn't get past the fact that the other reindeer weren't nice to Rudolph just because he was different. He was especially mad at the dad. I have watched the movie *Rudolf* for over 30 years and I never even picked up on the fact that it was Rudolf's dad who didn't defend him.

Roman analyzes *everything*! If a movie's story line is too foolish or doesn't make good sense, he will walk out of the theatre. As a result, there are very few movies in the theatre that he enjoys. I figure when he gets a little older he will be able to tolerate fantasy movies and not take everything so literally.

In another case, when Roman was four, my husband took him to the bookstore to read to him. He saw a boy playing with the store's train set display. Roman went up to the boy (who was thought to be around eight years old at the time) and said to him, "What's your name?"

The boy, who didn't want to be bothered by some little kid he didn't even know, dismissed him by saying, "Be quiet."

Roman, in his literalness, said, "Oh, hello, Be Quiet, do you want to play with me?"

"No, I don't," the boy said angrily.

Hurt and offended, Roman replied, "You know what, Be Quiet? You are *not* a nice boy!" and stormed off back to his father, who stood there disbelieving that Roman actually thought the boy's name was "Be Quiet."

He didn't address the issue at the time because he didn't want to hurt Roman's feelings, so he sat him down and read to him. As soon as they got home, Roman told me about the mean boy, "Be Quiet." I tried to explain to him that the boy's name couldn't be "Be Quiet," but he said, "Yes, it is. I asked him what his name was and he said 'Be Quiet.'" I was equally as shocked but let the issue go because I, too, didn't want to hurt his feelings even more by explaining to him that the boy was actually telling him to be quiet.

The following summer we were waiting at the airport en route to Boston to work at the camp. Waiting to board the plane was a man sitting quietly in a chair. He was of middle-eastern descent, with brown skin, a beard, shoulder-length wavy, dark brown hair, and wore a long robe-like garment and sandals. He sat there very statuesque and calm. When they called us to board the plane, the man stood up and Roman saw him. He exclaimed, "Oh my goodness! There's Jesus Christ!" and he ran over to the man.

I tried to grab him but it was too late. All the passengers getting ready to board looked at who he was pointing to and began laughing. Roman excitedly said, "Hello, Jesus! What are you doing here? Why aren't you in heaven?" The man chuckled and gently patted my poor naïve son's head. Embarrassed and taken aback, I firmly told him that he wasn't Jesus; he only looked like Jesus.

Roman rebuffed and in great detail explained, "It is Jesus! He's got long hair, a robe, sandals, and hair on his face, and big muscles, just like Jesus." I emphatically said that Jesus doesn't have big muscles. He argued and said, "Yes, He does, because He is mighty and strong and can hold the whole world in His hands!" (That idea comes from a song he sings at church, "He's got the whole world in His hands...")

I refused to debate this anymore with Roman and apologized to the man. He graciously said, "I've actually been told that I look like Jesus many times. You don't need to apologize; it's quite a compliment." I grabbed Roman so we could board the plane.

Tom, who is always reserved, was appalled by Roman's candor and ridiculousness. He whispered, "Honey, can't you do anything about this?"

"Oh, I'm sorry that I didn't know that he was going to announce to everyone that Jesus is here. Next time I'll put a gag over his mouth," I sarcastically replied.

Luckily we were some of the first ones to board the plane. We wanted to get out of that embarrassing situation as quickly as possible, only to find ourselves in another one. The plane we were boarding was a connecting flight, so there were already people on board who were continuing on to Boston. As soon as we walked down the aisle, Roman loudly announced to everyone on the plane, "Look, everybody! Jesus is going to ride the plane with us! Isn't that great? He's right behind us."

A man who was sipping his soda almost choked. They all began to laugh nervously because they thought the kid must be nuts. I told Roman to be quiet and sit down. Just then the man, a.k.a. "Jesus," boarded the plane so everyone understood and really laughed at what he was saying. "Soda man" graciously agreed and said, "He really does look like Jesus."

Roman quickly responded, "Oh, He is Jesus! He's just visiting from heaven." I quickly put my hand over his mouth before he could say anything else to derail our trip.

LOOK WHAT I CAN SEE!

Although Roman had conquered most of his behavioral, emotional, sensory, and autistic behaviors, there were still some quirky behaviors that he exhibited. In one area, having heightened sensory awareness was a wonderful asset for Roman. His visual perception was normal but was elevated by his hypersensitivity to sensations.

Roman has an acute visual awareness and is very detailed. He can see the most mundane things that most people would never be aware of. For example, if anything in a room or store had been changed or moved, he immediately noticed and inquired about where it went. He knew the logos of most stores and products. He would be the child to actually find a "needle in a haystack."

One day we went to see Santa Claus at Neiman Marcus. The store was splendidly decorated. It had a 50-foot Christmas tree displayed with over 3,000 tiny white lights. As soon as we approached the tree, Roman immediately told the salesman, "I love your Christmas tree, but one of the lights is not on." We all looked as he pointed way over to the bottom side of the tree where one miniature light was out, one amongst 3,000.

The salesman, who was taken aback and slightly perturbed by the small flaw in his meticulous display, said, "How on earth did you see that, and so quickly?"

While I subtlety tried to pull him away, our son, who has a penchant for the truth, proceeded to say, "You need to fix that light. The tree doesn't look right without it on."

The salesman just crossed his arms and huffed under his breath, "How rude!" and was most certainly pleased to see us leave.

I believe that Roman's heightened visual acuity enabled him

to read at an early age and also facilitated his ability to learn and associate things. He loves to build models because he likes the challenge of figuring out certain things.

According to Trott,

"Efficient processing of vestibular (sense of movement and gravity) information is strongly related to the ability to use visual information. It is the efficient integration of vestibular information that contributes to the understanding of spatial relationships. This understanding allows us to use left to right and top to bottom progression in such complex skills as reading, writing, and math."[15]

Chapter Fifteen

Aargh! Potty Training

Most children with autism or sensory dysfunction have an extremely difficult time with potty training, and our son was no exception. Aargh! This was the one skill I absolutely *dreaded* teaching Roman. It is difficult for children with autism or sensory problems to potty train because of their poor motor control and sensory perception. They do not have the same body awareness, nor do they feel the same way internally. Therefore when it is time for them to go to the bathroom, they may not feel the urge. Their processing system is totally different. When they stim they are looking at something, they can see a cause and effect, and it is visually pleasing to them. When they have a bowel movement, they don't like the feeling or may not care and cannot visually see as it is happening. Therefore it may be uncomfortable or frightening for them, or they might not even notice that it has happened.

I can usually heed wise counsel and am never too proud to ask for help or say "I don't know." I consider this a positive attribute. Wise counsel is when you learn from the wisdom and knowledge of others who have gone through some of your same experiences and then apply it to your own situation.

One day when Roman was two I met a woman at the park who was with her six-year-old son. We were the only ones there that day so we began casually talking. She told me about a disability her son had been healed from a year earlier. She said, "My son had a problem called Sensory Processing Disorder. I know you never heard of it but…"

I anxiously interrupted in complete astonishment, "Yes! Oh Lord, yes, I have heard of it. My son has it, too!" We couldn't believe the coincidence. What are the chances of the only people in the entire park both dealing with the same problem? She explained how her son was healed because of all the therapies she did with him. I saw how well her son talked, played, and interacted, and was amazed at how perfectly fine he was. I would never have been able to tell that there was ever anything wrong with him.

I told her Roman still had so many problems to overcome. She encouraged me to just keep working with him and then gave me some unsolicited advice that was extremely beneficial to me. She explained that children with disabilities often have a hard time learning how to potty train. She advised me not to even begin potty training until he turned three. Then she told me not to teach him to poop on the potty until he turned four.

I exclaimed, "Four years old! What?" I had never heard of a child not being potty trained by four and thought to myself, "Do they even have pull-ups for kids that old?" I contemplated that maybe this lady just might be a little crazy. After all, I didn't know who she was or anything about her. She went on to explain how kids with disabilities may need an extra year to get better control of their bodies, and that I will only frustrate myself and my son if I try it before then.

I asked her why so late as four? She didn't offer any scientific or professional reason, only that once they turn four they just "get it." I listened to what she had to say and then observed her well-adjusted and fully healed son. I said to myself, "Listen to someone who has had success. She's trying to help you. After all, that was the only thing she said that sounded off balance. She's only trying to make your life a little easier." I hesitantly said, "Well, okay. I won't do it until he is four." End of story; I didn't question her anymore or stress about it.

Of course, when I called my mother and told her what this perfect stranger had said, she thought she was nuts. (My dear, sweet mom who, bless her heart, patiently bore with me through my daily dribbles about Roman's progress and regress; I constantly sought her advice and encouragement. We usually were in agreement, but not in this case.)

She nearly exploded when I told her about waiting to potty train. She yelled, "Four years old! I've never heard of such! He'll practically be in college! I had five kids and all of you were potty trained by two. There's no child in the world that isn't potty trained by four!"

I knew she was only trying to help, but I didn't listen to her; she never had a child with this problem. I had to listen to the wise counsel of someone who had been through this and was successful. After all, you don't ask a homeless person how to make money; you seek the advice from a millionaire who has had success.

Needless to say, I didn't make the year of the "terrible two's" anymore terrible by adding the additional drudgery of potty training. Besides, when I went to the store I saw that they did indeed make pull-ups for toddlers up to age five. So I guess my son wasn't going to be the only four-year-old in the whole world still being potty trained.

As soon as Roman turned three, I explained that it was time for him to learn to go on the potty. We did a month of potty prep time. I repeatedly read potty books to him and showed him *The Potty Movie* for boys and bought the *Sesame Street* potty seat. With just a couple of accidents, a few weeks later he was completely potty trained for peeing. He felt very little anxiety or stress, and neither did I. I only had him put on a pull-up at night just in case he had an accident. Every night I woke him up around midnight so he could go potty, and this stopped him from ever having an accident in the bed.

As soon as he turned four, I told him it was time to poop in the potty. After I convinced him that he wasn't going to be flushed away with the poop, it took him only a few days to be completely potty trained. The lady at the park was right. I would have never known to do this had she not told me. I never did see her again. It was as if God put her there to give me that little piece of advice that no one else had ever told me. That saved me from a year of struggling to get him potty trained.

Chapter Sixteen

Family Reunions

When Roman turned four, he was dismissed from all school services and was officially no longer on the autism spectrum. There are still some remnants of this disorder that will always be with him, but I cannot express the depth of the sense of accomplishment and inner satisfaction I felt due to his tremendous achievements.

We had attained all of our goals and my checklist was about 99% complete. Now it was time for the official unveiling of him to my Boston family members, whom we had not seen in two years. My mother had seen him because she had often come to visit and offer her support. The last time his uncles, aunts, and cousins saw Roman was at my father's funeral when he had just turned two and was in the midst of his autistic symptoms. When we left Boston, I didn't know when we would actually see any of them again. They offered me their prayers and wished me good luck. I knew they felt sorry for him and were uncertain if he would ever get better.

Two years later we all met in Chicago for a special event at Northwestern University. My father, four brothers, and I are all Northwestern graduates, and this was the siblings' first time being together again. They didn't know what to expect when they saw Roman, and, needless to say, they were amazed at the results. Roman approached them, gave them all hugs, and articulately said, "It's a pleasure to see you again, my wonderful family. Did you all have a nice plane ride?"

The last time they saw him he couldn't even say "Hi." He engaged them in conversation and was warm, witty, and charming. My whole family was delighted by his recovery. My brother Steven, who I yelled at two years prior for his insensitive comments, came over to me shaking his head in amazement and said, "Unbelievable! What did you do to him? How did you do it? He's not even the same kid!"

He gave me a hug and told me how proud he was of me and how absolutely awesome Roman was. Throughout the years I had explained to my family all that we had been through, but Steven said that he had no idea how serious his condition really was and how sorry he had been.

BLACK-TIE AFFAIR

When Roman was five years old we took him to Boston for a formal dinner at Gillette Stadium, home of the New England Patriots, to raise money for our camp. To me it felt just like a scene right out of the movie classic *My Fair Lady* when Henry Higgins teaches a socially inept, impoverished, uneducated flower girl, Eliza Doolittle, how to speak and behave properly and is able to pass her off as royalty at a grand ball.

There were over 500 people attending, many of whom were successful, distinguished businessmen and women. Roman looked so handsome dressed in his boy's tuxedo, and we proudly took him around the dining room where he cordially and formally greeted many of the people. The guests there had no idea that there had ever been anything wrong with him.

He worked the room with ease and properly exchanged hellos and pleasantries. He patiently sat at the dinner table with me for three hours and entertained himself by coloring houses and writing stories. He appropriately conversed with the guests at our table. Because he was so young, they were impressed by his conversation and his ability to sit quietly for so long. At the end of the dinner, we introduced our son and he came up to the microphone in front of 500 people and confidently said, "It's such a pleasure to be here tonight. I hope everyone had a great time." And just like no one at the ball ever figured out that Eliza wasn't royalty, no one at the formal dinner ever surmised that Roman had autism.

'TWAS THE MORNING OF CHRISTMAS...

As I reflect on my lowest and most challenging moments, such as "the abyss," I can fully appreciate just how far Roman has come. I am also reminded that there were also many endearing and sweet moments; we weren't always in crisis mode.

At two years of age, Roman was often in a state of turmoil, but one thing that calmed him was Christmas lights and displays. Every evening in December, Tom and I drove him around several neighborhoods so he could see the awesome Christmas displays on the all the homes. I brought hot chocolate and cookies, and he squealed with delight as he listened to Christmas carols and viewed all the brightly colored displays. They absolutely captivated him and brought a sense of calmness and peace to his world. Many nights I didn't feel like driving the same hour-long route, but this was a positive ritual that eventually manifested an unusual event.

My husband, Tom, works in the computer industry and each year he and his fellow employees take turns working the holiday shifts. The Christmas Eve when Roman was four, Tom had to work from 7:00 that night until 7:00 the next morning.

Roman awoke early Christmas morning at 5:00 to see what treasures Santa had brought. He ran down the stairs to awaken me and we scurried into the living room to the Christmas tree. Just as it is for every child on Christmas morn, it is magical to him. He just couldn't wait to dive into those presents. I told him to get his stocking and we could soon begin opening gifts.

Much to my dismay he said, "Oh no, Mommy. We can't open the presents until Daddy gets home." I told him that Daddy wouldn't be coming home for a few more hours. Roman didn't flinch when he calmly said, "Okay, then we'll wait."

I stopped in my tracks. "Are you serious?" I asked in shock. "Surely you don't want to wait that long to open your presents."

Roman said, "Oh yes, Mommy. We need to open them as a family. That's what Christmas is all about. I don't mind waiting, but I will open my stocking."

At that moment, time changed hands. In Roman I could now see myself, not so much in the struggle, but in the recovery. I saw myself waiting, not restlessly as one would imagine, but as patient as someone who realizes that all of life's gifts sit right before him, all within his reach. I knew firsthand how someone could wait patiently for something so valuable to him.

That boy sat in front of the tree for three hours waiting for his daddy to come home so he could share with him what he deemed to be the special moment of opening the gifts. He joyfully said, "Let's just sit in front of the tree and listen to Christmas carols and eat Christmas candy while we wait."

So I lit a warm fire and Christmas candles, and he sat beside me on the couch, listening to Christmas carols and admiring all the beautifully wrapped gifts. When he spotted the biggest gift hidden behind the tree, he said, "Look, Mommy, at that big, beautiful present! I hope it's for me."

When Tom walked through the door at 7:45, Roman ran into his arms saying, "Daddy, you're home! Now we can open the presents!"

Tom couldn't believe that Roman actually waited all that time for him to come home before he opened his gifts. He sighed, "That's the best gift of all."

I surmise that during all those drives down those cold, Christmas-lit streets a bonding was taking place. Having recovered from the autism, all the Christmas rituals we had done in the past meant so much to him. I believe the time we spent together driving around looking at the beautiful lights and displays resulted in him wanting us all to be together when he opened the gifts. It was one of many memories we would guard in our newfound lives, another example of God's grace and mercy. We were grateful and relieved beyond measure.

Chapter Seventeen

Raindrops on Roman

I still had one last problem on my checklist to conquer, and that was getting Roman to put his head under water so he could learn how to swim. He did not like to stand in the rain because he did not like raindrops falling on his head. He loved taking baths, but was afraid to take showers because, again, water was falling on his head. He was terrified of putting his head under water. Swimming was the only activity he was afraid of that I delayed working on. It simply wasn't a skill he needed for social or educational purposes. But if he was ever going to learn how to swim, he had to conquer his fear of putting his head under water.

When Roman was two and three years old, he would not stand in the two-foot shallow end of an in-ground pool. I would stand in front of him with my arms extended, encouraging him to get in, but he had these irrational fears. He said, "But there's no bottom and I'll sink."

Impatient and bewildered, I tried to reason with him and adamantly declared, "Roman, of course there's a bottom. I am standing on the bottom! Look at my feet; they're on the pool floor! You won't go under."

"That's because you're tall."

"Look at all the other kids in the pool! They aren't sinking!"

"That's because they're magical." He wasn't joking either.

Many children with sensory issues perceive things differently. Try as I might, there was no convincing him. Not wanting to deal with this particular issue at the time, I rationalized and thought to myself that he didn't have to learn to swim just yet. I knew I would eventually have to tackle this problem, and I didn't want to wait too much longer because it would only become more difficult.

Then one day when Roman turned four, just like in the case of the potty training, it clicked. He suddenly had a desire to learn how to swim. One of his best friends, Yates, could swim like a fish, and Roman wanted to swim like him. He was learning to perceive things more accurately and was becoming less fearful. He was finally able to put his feet on what he could finally see was the bottom of the pool.

I contacted a swim teacher named Ms. Autumn. She had taught swimming for 30 years and assured me that she could teach anyone how to swim, including kids with special needs. I told her about Roman's issues and the fact that he wouldn't put his head under water. She gave me wise counsel and advised me on a few techniques to use before he began swim lessons.

Ms. Autumn told me to take a handful of water and sprinkle a little on his head when he was taking a bath, allowing him to get used to the water running down his face. Once he felt comfortable with water coming down on his face, I had to splash water on his head and in his face. I explained to Roman what I was going to do and at first he was fearful and jumped away. I told him that if he was going to learn how to swim, he had to put his head in the water. I repeated the water prep time over and over again, and he was actually beginning to like it. I did this every night for a month. I knew he was ready when I was able to fill up a small bucket of water and actually pour it over his head without it bothering him.

Roman also had to learn to blow bubbles in the water. At first he only touched his lips in the water. Then he gradually went from lips to chin, and finally his whole face, but not his whole head. I decided that was something Ms. Autumn would have to contend with. Getting his face into the water was a major milestone, and Roman was actually looking forward to swim lessons.

I knew I was on a roll and had to take advantage of it. If Roman could tolerate the water in his face, it was time to get him into the shower. He resisted at first, but I slowly had him reach just his arms in and let them get wet; then I did the same with his legs. I turned the showerhead away a little so it was not coming down directly on him when he stood in the shower. Once he was in, he began to like it. I slowly turned the showerhead so just a little water came down on his head. When he was comfortable with that, all bets were off. Roman was finally taking a shower. It took four years, but who's counting?

Do you see how tedious this all is? What is easily teachable to the typical child is like climbing Mount Everest for children with autism. Many tasks that I thought should only take three steps to do often took my child 463 steps to do!

It doesn't rain that much in Texas, but whenever a rainstorm came I took Roman outside and let the rain fall on his head while we sang songs like "Raindrops on Roman and whiskers on kittens..." and "Raindrops keep falling on my head..." and he actually enjoyed it. I know we looked foolish; most moms tell their kids to come in out of the rain, and I told mine to go stand in it.

A month later he began swimming lessons, and, true to her word, by the time the swimming session was over she had taught him to swim.

If I wasn't there to see it for myself, I wouldn't have believed it. On the first day she got him to completely put his face under water.

Why? We prepared him. We told him what to expect and got his face used to the water. In three weeks Roman could actually swim across the pool with his head in the water, only coming up for breaths when necessary. By the end of the lessons, he could swim the entire length of the pool. My husband couldn't believe it. He had to come to the lessons to see for himself! This is a perfect example of the old adage, "Preparation and practice can indeed make perfect!"

It is for these reasons that I write my story. With the irrational fears and perceptions Roman had, this was a feat I would have thought impossible. I didn't even dare to dream that he would learn to swim during his first set of lessons. So I implore all the parents of babies and toddlers with autism to be an advocate for your child. Find the therapies and treatments that you feel will most effectively meet the needs of your child.

Roman overcame 45 autistic and sensory problems. He even learned how to swim! A month prior to his lessons, he couldn't even put his face in the water. See all the accomplishments! Make them happen for your child! So much of this is on you and what you can enable them to achieve.

CHAPTER EIGHTEEN

A Time for Camaraderie

One thing that Roman has been blessed with is being surrounded by kind and loving people. Since moving to Dallas, I always bragged that we had to be living in one of the friendliest cities I had ever been in. Just about everyone I've met since moving here ten years ago has been extraordinarily pleasant.

STRANGER DANGER

When Roman was four, however, I tried to teach him about stranger danger and that all people aren't nice; he refused to believe me. He would adamantly rebuff, "Everyone is nice mommy; don't say such horrible things about people!"

One positive aspect of children with autism (like many children with special needs) is that most of them have such sweet, untainted spirits.

Often times they are more sensitive and compassionate than the "typical" child. When we go shopping or run errands, Roman is quick to say hello to everyone and tell them to have a blessed day.

One day a little girl whom he didn't know was eating an ice-cream cone and Roman went up to her and said, "That wonderful chocolate ice-cream cone with colored sprinkles sure does look scrumptious. And the colored sprinkles on your ice cream match the colored polka dots on your shirt." She just looked at him and smiled because she didn't know how to respond. Roman just has an extra-friendly nature and believes everyone is a friend. But don't mistake his kindness for weakness. He will defend anyone whom he feels is being wronged, including himself.

On the other hand, because he is so trusting, I had to repeatedly tell him that not everyone is good and that he would have to be more discerning. My mother kept saying, "You have to make him understand about strangers." I told her not to be so worried about it, until one day I knew I had to do something.

One afternoon when Roman was three years old, our doorbell rang. We had always told Roman to never answer the door unless Mommy or Daddy was with him. Tom was at work and I had gone in to take a shower and didn't hear the doorbell. Roman opened the door and a salesman asked if his mother was home. He said, "Sure is. Come on in."

The man remained in the foyer while Roman came and knocked on our bedroom door and said, "Mommy, someone's here." I couldn't hear him because the shower was on and asked him what he had said. He responded, "Oh, never mind, I'll wait." So I took my dear sweet time showering and getting dressed and came out of the room a few minutes later to find some stranger sitting on my living room couch having a conversation with Roman.

I was stunned! I exclaimed, "Who are you?"

He was friendly in his reply and said, "Oh, I'm a salesman wanting to know if you are interested in…" I didn't even listen to what it was he was trying to sell. I just wanted him out of my house. He said that Roman was great to talk with and that he told him he wanted to be an architect when he grows up. I just couldn't believe that my son let a perfect stranger into my house. I told him that I didn't know he was here and apologized for the wait, then immediately told him I wasn't interested and escorted him out of our home.

It was then that I told Roman emphatically about strangers and how dangerous it was for him to do that. "But he's not a stranger; he was nice," he defended. This time I refused to relent. When Tom came home we practiced with Roman what he should do when strangers came to the door, and he learned then that he was never to open the door again unless we were there beside him.

DAY TRIPS

Day trips to places like the zoo, library, gardens, farms, aquarium, nature walks, and museums are excellent for the development of language and social skills. It is a great learning experience to let him see in person many of the things that he has seen in books.

Make sure to do day-trip prep time by reading a book about the place you will be visiting so he will know what to expect and will be excited about it. Engage in language drills by encouraging him to pronounce words or use sentences to tell about all the different things he will see. Ask questions like, "What animal is that?" Make sure he answers with a complete sentence if he is fluent, like "That is a tiger." If he is just beginning to learn to talk, one-word answers are fine. Day trips also teach social skills by making him behave in an appropriate way out in society. This also can be a nice enjoyable break for you.

Make sure to plan well before you go. If his needs are met, it will make for a successful trip. Whenever I took Roman on a day trip (for instance, to the zoo), I always had my husband with me for any extra assistance I might need. We always went early before it became too crowded or too hot. I made sure Roman was well rested, packed enough snacks and drinks for him, and brought a variety of extra clothes, just in case of temperature change (because this affected his sensory system). When he began to tire after a few hours, we left while he was still in the enjoyment phase. I always had our day trips meticulously planned; therefore they were a complete success.

CHAPTER NINETEEN

Roman Today

By the time he was four, Roman had completely overcome his autistic and sensory problems and was no longer testing on the autism spectrum. I believe that all the work of the therapists, the skills and drills program that I instituted, along with the power of prayer are what helped heal our son. Whereas he used to run 50 and 60 laps around our living room, he now uses his running ability to play on basketball and soccer teams. Roman has been back at our camp for the past two years, and although he is too young to actually be a camper, he is able to participate in much of the training that the campers do.

Along with all of the ridiculousness and longsuffering, there was an equal amount of good that resulted from this disorder. I was able to extract the good from the bad and change the negative behaviors, like the stimming, sensory issues, and behavioral problems, by redirecting and turning them into something positive.

One advantage that may go along with this disorder is the intellectual capabilities of some children with autism. I realized early on that Roman could learn and memorize quickly and retain information at a very young age. I believe that all the skills and drills only helped stimulate his brain, making it easier for him to learn. I had him do skills that were for *his* developmental age. (The developmental age is the level at which a child is able to succeed in a skill or activity. It is not the same as chronological age. The child's ability, not birth date, determines a child's developmental age.)

By the age of two, Roman knew the entire alphabet, the numbers one to ten, and all the shapes and colors. At age three he learned how to read, knew many concept skills, such as rhyming and sequencing, and knew all the days of the week and months of the year. At four he learned how to add and subtract. By age five he learned how to tell time, and he also learned how to write complete sentences.

All of the work we did in the skills and drills program has made Roman confident and has given him a joy of learning. This was important because I wanted to minimize any frustration he might have in school. I'm not telling you this to boast, but to show you the results of our work and what the possibilities could be for many children. The skills and drills program can be used for any child. I believe that *all* babies and toddlers can benefit from an early, consistent, structured learning program.

It's A Wonderful Life...School

Due to the fact that Roman had to overcome such tremendous odds, we chose to be extremely selective as to where he would attend school. Because of the "abyss" incident, I knew he had to be in a peaceful, loving, and disciplined environment. Fortunately, we were able to find an outstanding charter school called Life School.

Life School teaches students how to excel in every area of their lives. They are exemplary in their academics and also equally committed to teaching students how to have sterling character. One of Life School's strongest points is that it doesn't tolerate any bullying, foul language, or disruptive behaviors. Being around appropriate and positive behavior is very important because developing proper socialization skills is a vital part of overcoming autism.

Life School has an excellent disciplinary system that holds students accountable. They teach them to be respectful and to put others before themselves. As a result of these high ethical standards, the students have high self-esteem, strive to achieve their best, and are extremely well-behaved. Good company elevates good character, and this positive educational environment has only augmented Roman's confidence, allowing him to accomplish all the expectations I had for him. In other words, we have found an extended family.

This school has such a commendable reputation that parents have to actually camp out overnight in order to get their child enrolled there. My husband Tom was given that task. He slept outside in a lounge chair along with hundreds of other parents, with temperatures dipping below 30 degrees that night. I dare say it was well worth it. Something worthwhile is worth waiting for, and that is what recovery is all about.

The principal and staff of Life School expect great things and assure their students they can do great things, thus allowing them to achieve great things. I wish every school was run with this kind of integrity, discipline, and love. I believe that this school could be the model for every public school to emulate.

On the last day of the school year, Life School has a wonderful awards ceremony, rewarding students for outstanding academics and character. Roman was the recipient of the Citizenship Award, an award earned by the student that demonstrates leadership in "putting others first, and doing unto others as you would have them do unto you." I was extremely proud and honored. There are many children there with outstanding character who could have won this award. For him to have won is incredible, given the odds against him; this award exemplifies how far he has come.

I've always believed there is something in a name that is important, and Life School illustrates that. Life is a learning experience that reaches far beyond four walls. For some, it may be a life of hard knocks, for others a walk in the park. But for those of us who are experiencing autism, life is a journey through uncharted water. You must be careful to surround your child with positive things – things that enhance your child's development – and this is what Life School is all about.

REMNANTS OF AUTISM

Most of the effects I see from Roman's autism today are

positive. Roman is very kind and compassionate towards others and is extremely agreeable and polite. The repetition of all the social skills truly paid off. Roman can meet, greet, and talk to people with ease. He would like to be an architect one day and will sit for hours at his desk, drawing and building houses and constructing various Lego models with incredible precision and detail.

One remnant of Roman's autism is that he continues to have difficulty eating some foods. I still have to cut most of his food into small pieces. He also has some oral defensiveness with food and continues to have a very limited repertoire of what he will eat. The positive side to this is that most of the foods he will eat are healthy, and it doesn't cost a lot to feed him. The other remnants are that he is very literal, sensitive, and cautious; therefore I have to be more protective of his environment and exposure.

Many children have some difficulty adjusting to the adolescent years. For Roman and other children with special needs, the adjustment may be more difficult. Therefore, it is important that they stay under the umbrella of their diagnosis. Doing so enables the child to receive the services the state provides for his specific needs. These particular students are what I consider "gray-area" students; they do not require special education, but at some point they may need a specific service. For this reason it is important that these services remain available to them.

When Roman entered kindergarten, I enrolled him in the Individuals with Disabilities Education Improvement Act (IDEIA). IDEIA is a federally funded state program that provides services for all children with disabilities. All states are required to provide free education that meets the specific and appropriate needs of the child. I feel having this service is necessary and important if any future assistance is needed. As I previously stated, Roman does not need any of these services at this point, but IDEIA allows the "gray-area" students who could fall through the cracks to maintain their eligibility for services.

CHAPTER TWENTY

Conclusion

I designed a methodical skills and drills program to meet the specific needs of my child. There is no objective scientific evidence to support why my skills and drills program worked; I only know that it was successful. I ascertained Roman's problems and devised the skills to combat those issues. What I wish to convey is how all of his problems either faded away or were transformed into positive traits that now benefit his life.

There is no known cure for autism but, because of Roman's success, I sincerely believe there are many more babies and toddlers who stand a chance at recovery. I wish to share my skills and drills with parents who are going through similar circumstances. The goal of recovery is attainable, but parents have to be willing to put in the effort. Many children may not improve as quickly or attain full recovery, but if you take the time to develop them to *their* fullest potential, you and your child will receive the blessings God has for you.

I believe that my inner drive and steadfastness is perhaps innate, passed down from parents who refused to give up. Both of my parents worked hard and built a successful sports camp to help children. My father, the late Ron Burton, came from a very poor family and achieved tremendous academic, athletic, and professional accomplishments.

My mother was a homemaker and was instrumental in helping all of us achieve our educational goals. My youngest brother, Paul, had dyslexia, and she made sure he received all the special educational services and skills he needed to compensate for his disability. Today Paul has two master's degrees and a doctorate; he is now an associate pastor and a news reporter for a major television station in Boston. I use my brother Paul as an example to show how his special needs were met and resulted in tremendous achievements.

I know my utter determination and resolve came from my deep faith in Christ and the inner drive and perseverance I learned from my parents. All of these attributes helped me win the battle for our son's life.

I conclude my story with the words of my late father, the wonderful Ron Burton. He often used these words of encouragement at the end of his motivational speeches. "Good luck, God bless, and may the wind always, always, be at your back."

Dear Parents:

It is with the utmost respect and reverence that I thank God, because no man can offer the amount of support one needs to get through this, and it is unfair to even expect it of anyone. For three years I endured what required the patience of a saint, one of which I am not. I often looked to the Bible to find something, anything that would give me the sense of hope that I needed to endure. Autism is like a mountain that is not first seen. As you are walking, it appears that you are on a level playing field, but when you look up, a mountain suddenly appears. But you can't let the mountain stop you. You have to cross over to the other side, because there is where you will find peace, comfort, and healing. In Philippians 4:13 it says, "I can do all things through Christ who strengthens me." He imparted to me the wisdom and fortitude to fight and win the war against autism.

Autism is so consuming that it is life-altering. It consumes every thought you have and everything you do. It requires a relentless amount of sacrifice, but we are sacrificing for the good of our children. If time is what you seek, there is none. Do not lend a blind eye to what you feel in your heart to be true. If you know in your heart that something is not right with your child, you must act upon it, because with autism, time is not your friend.

There's a song called "Why Me, Lord?" The lyrics begin, "What have I ever done to deserve even one of the blessings you've shown?" I now look at this whole journey as a blessing. I am a new person, one filled with more love, compassion, and understanding. I've witnessed miracles and now want to offer others hope. This story is our message of hope. Hope is the lifeline of all life's obstacles. Grab and hold on to it and never give up, so that you can be uplifted from what appears to be, from every angle, an abyss.

After all of this, I can't tell you what to believe in. I just know that you have to believe in something in order to be a believer. Just as the Bible may take a person a lifetime to fully interpret or understand, so, too, can autism. But while you are waiting, you can't be still; you must be proactive. I pray everyday for my son, my husband, myself, and all of you. I am grateful that our son has experienced restoration, and my prayer is now that every child with autism will as well.

Appendix I

Skills and Drills Supplies

The "Skills and Drills" program can be used for all preschool children. Every child can benefit from a consistent, structured early learning program. It can increase a child's intellectual and learning capabilities, and will give them a "yearning for learning." There are a multitude of skills and drills I did with Roman to meet his specific needs. The following is a list of *all* the skills and drills we did. Once you see these skills, you will have a better understanding of why Roman's recovery process was so successful. The skills and drills were multi-sensory tasks, meaning many senses were involved in each task. We developed and stimulated every part of his brain and all of his senses, which was critical for his recovery. I have listed all the language skills, fine and gross motor skills, and tactile, sensory, and academic skills. Each day we alternated different table and floor activities so they would not become monotonous and Roman would have an opportunity to explore and learn new things.

In the beginning the skills, drills, and therapy were often cumbersome but were eventually very rewarding. I implemented a well-organized program that ultimately became enjoyable for both of us. In order to make the program run smoothly, I gathered all of the materials I used in an organized fashion. I stored all the small toys in labeled containers and boxes and designated a certain area of our home to be used solely for storage. This made it easy to quickly find and get to the things I needed and eased the transition from one activity to the next.

I had a recognized "clean-up" time and assisted Roman in putting away any supplies used. It was important to teach him to clean up and put things away after each activity. I did not begin another skill before putting away the supplies for the previous one. I tried to keep our home fairly neat and organized, thus making it less complicated to commence the next activity. A C-R-S (Consistent, Repetitive, and Structured) program helped Roman to remain on task, focus, and master the skills.

In *all* of the skills I incorporated lots of language. He had to describe or explain what he was doing in each activity. If he didn't know what to say, I provided him with a sentence or word and had him repeat it. For example: "I am playing with the dog." "Let's go through the tunnel." "I can beat the drum." "I like to color." I had Roman engage in conversations throughout the entire day along with his skills and drills, and it became natural and fun. This was one of the most efficient methods of increasing his language skills.

When I first began, Roman's sit-time, or his ability to stay on task, was minimal. I began with 30 seconds to one minute per skill. Because I did this consistently everyday, over the next few months his sit-time substantially increased because he was learning how to stay focused. He began to enjoy doing the skills and drills and ultimately learned how to play effectively and complete each activity.

The only significant cost of Roman's therapy for my family was for purchasing the toys and supplies. Most of the supplies I purchased at Target,

Wal-Mart, Dollar Store, Michael's Crafts, and Hobby Lobby. The following is a list of toys and supplies you will need for an effective skills and drills program. For the table skills you will need a small table and chairs. For the floor skills you can use a large area rug. The rug is not a necessity, but it makes floor-time more comfortable and it defines a designated area for floor skills.

Table Skills Supplies:

- play dough kit
- alphabet letters
- numbers 1-10
- table puzzles: animals, transportation, shapes, etc.
- coloring books
- white construction paper
- concept skill cards/flashcards: rhyming, sequencing, matching, opposites
- lots of children's picture books (library, Half-Price Books)
- multi-colored balloon poster board

Fine Motor Skills Supplies: (Done at table or on floor)

- arts and craft supplies: glue, washable markers and paint, paint brushes, finger paint, washable crayons, scissors, glitter, cotton balls, pom-poms, foamies, shaving cream, stickers, stamps, stamp pad
- snap beads
- lacing (pictures)
- fine motor puzzles: buttoning, zipping, snapping
- wooden beads
- rainbow peg play
- squeeze toys and balls
- stacking cups/ small blocks
- toy instruments
- echo mike
- popsicle sticks
- easel
- blocks: wooden, cardboard, pop-on, mega blocks

Gross Motor Skills Supplies: (Done on floor)

- toddler basketball hoop and basketball
- toy bowling set
- floor balance beam (purchase at Home Depot – long piece of wood 4-6 inches in width)
- small ball
- tunnel
- hula hoop
- bean bag toss
- ring toss
- therapy ball

Floor Skills Supplies:

- costumes/dress up
- shape sorter
- bubbles
- camera with flash
- play food
- toy cordless or cell phone
- view finder
- blocks
- kits for imaginative play: farm, doctor, circus, builder, tea, play ground, school yard, castle

Keep these toys organized in a toy chest, on shelves, or in containers. Make sure your child cleans up and puts away all toys and supplies in a designated area. This will maintain order for you and him and will make playtime simple and enjoyable.

Skills and Drills Lessons

A note on floor time: It is important that you are down on the floor with him during floor time for natural and imaginative floor play where he can be eye to eye with you, because you are giving him visual cues and teaching attention to task. Use kits of things that are real in their lives for imaginative play, such as a doctor's kit, tea set, builder kit, vehicles set, or school, farm, circus, zoo, or airport kits. This play allows him to be in charge of the action and skills and vocabulary as they use a variety of objects that apply to that setting, career, or place.

A. Language Skills: (1-19)

"All language, verbal, nonverbal, and written requires the most complex integration of sensory and motor information. It is an abstraction of personal experiences, and the ability to share and relate to experiences is essential in developing relationships with others."[16]

1. Alphabet Drills:

Use a set of upper-case alphabet letters. Begin with the letter "A." Say to him, "This is the letter "A." Can you say "A?" Do the alphabet in order. Point to the letter and try and have him repeat it.

Then have him point to the letter and try to say it. Have him hold the letter. Introduce one letter each day or week, depending on how fast he learns. Keep a list of each letter he says. Make sure he learns that letter before you go on to the next. If he can't say it, make sure he knows it by having him point to it. Make sure you review all the letters he has learned each day. Use a letters puzzle. Have him place letters in the puzzle.

Develops/Improves: Language; letter matching, selection and recognition; eye-hand coordination; spatial relations skills.

2. Numbers Drills:

Use a set of numbers one through nine. Begin with number one. Say to him, "This is the number one. Can you say one?" Point to the number and encourage him to repeat it. Then have him point to the number and try to say it. Have him hold the number. Keep a list of each number he says. Introduce one number each day or week, depending on how fast he learns. Make sure he learns that number before you go on to the next. If he can't say it, make sure he knows it by having him point to it. Make sure you review all the numbers he has learned each day. Use a numbers puzzle. Have him place the numbers into the puzzle.

Develops/Improves: Language; number matching, selection and recognition; eye-hand coordination; spatial relations skills.

3. Word Chart:

Make a word chart of all the words he learns how to say. Have him repeat all the words each day in order for him to really learn and remember how to say them. Add to the word chart with each new word he says. This will be exciting and encouraging for you and him.

Develops/Improves: Language, memory, and auditory processing skills.

4. Reading:

Get books that teach about things in their world, such as the alphabet, numbers, shapes, colors, animals, nature, farm, school, park, transportation, circus, zoo, parks, holidays, and sports. Have him sit in front of you on the floor and read him a book. Point to various pictures and encourage him to say what is in the picture. It is important that he learns how to sit and focus during story time. Read one to four books to him everyday.

Develops/Improves: Language, vocabulary, memory, concentration, and attention span.

5. Touch and Feel Books:

Read an assortment of textured books. Have him touch and feel the variety of surfaces and textures in the books. Name the different textures, such as soft, wooly, hairy, bumpy, furry, spongy, silky, rubbery, shiny, scratchy, and smooth. Have him say the word associated with different pictures and textures in the book.

Develops/Improves: Language, vocabulary, sensory awareness, and discrimination skills.

6. Flash Cards:

Use an assortment of flash cards. Have him try to say the word associated with the picture on the flash card.

Develops/Improves: Language, vocabulary, and visual recognition skills.

7. Sing-Along:

Sing nursery rhyme songs, such as "Row Your Boat," "Twinkle Little Star," "Head, Shoulders, Knees, and Toes," "Wheels on the Bus," and "Humpty Dumpty." Use hand gestures while singing. Have him play his instruments while you sing together.

Develops/Improves: Language, vocabulary, rhyming words, fine motor skills, manual dexterity, and eye-hand coordination skills.

8. Telephone Talk:

Pretend to call him on a play cell phone and teach him to talk into the phone. Ask him questions like, "Who is this?" "How are you today?" "What are you going to do today?" Tell him what to say for the answers. This helps him to learn how to talk on the phone and talk in complete 3-4 word sentences.

Develops/Improves: Language and socialization skills.

9. Activity Picture Cards:

Show real pictures of children's everyday routines, activities, and play, such as a child playing on the computer, playing baseball, sleeping, fishing, or riding a bike. Have him describe what the child is doing in the picture in complete sentences. "The boy is painting." "He is brushing his teeth." "She is reading a book." "They are playing soccer." "She is swimming." Place several cards in front of him. Ask a question about one of the cards and have him point to the correct card. For example: "Which child is eating?"

Develops/Improves: Language, thinking, and pronoun usage.

10. Sequencing Cards:

Place three-piece pictures of everyday activities and routines in sequence. Tell him to describe which goes first, next, and last in order using complete sentences.

Develops/Improves: Language, thinking, and visual sequencing skills.

11. Classifying Cards:

Sort cards into groups of three things that go together. Classify cards into specific groups, such as toys, vehicles, animals, tools, foods, or playground equipment. Have him say words associated with the pictures of each group of cards.

Develops/Improves: Language, vocabulary, classification skills, thinking, and visual perception skills.

12. Puzzles:

Use a variety of floor and table puzzles to teach about all the different places, objects, and things he needs to know that apply to his world: types of animals (pets, farm, wild, zoo, and ocean animals), shapes, parks, transportation, instruments, food, nature, rainforests, tools, and the human body. Encourage him to talk about and point to different puzzle pieces, then have him place them in the correct spot.

Develops/Improves: Language, vocabulary, fine motor skills, eye-hand coordination, and spatial relations skills.

13. Learning Colors:

Using a poster of different colored balloons, teach him all the colors. Point to each one and name the color. Point to the blue balloon and say, "This is the blue balloon." Then ask him, "Which one is the blue balloon?" Have him point to it. Then go on to the next color. Teach one color each day or week, depending on how quickly he learns. Try and have him pronounce the word for each color. Always encourage him to say the initial consonant sounds, like "b" for blue. Go over the colors he has already learned to make ensure that he remembers them. Then go on to the next color. Complete all primary colors. Keep going over the colors with him each day.

Develops/Improves: Language, thinking, and color recognition skills.

14. Learning Shapes:

Get a puzzle containing a circle, square, and triangle. Name the shapes. Have him point to and pick up the shapes and place then into the puzzle. Once mastered, teach more shapes with an eight-piece puzzle.

Develops/Improves: Shape discrimination and recognition, fine motor skills, eye-hand coordination, and spatial relations skills.

15. Shape Sorter:

Place different shapes in front of him and have him point to the various shapes by name and have him place the shapes into the correct slots.

Develops/Improves: Language, shape discrimination and recognition, fine motor skills, eye-hand coordination, and spatial relations skills.

16. Play Animals:

Get sets of farm, wild, and pet animals. Teach him the names of the animals and the sounds they make. Categorize them into farm, wild, and pet animals. Have him hold the animals and move them around. Play "find the animal" – let him watch as you hide an animal behind a toy or under a pillow and ask "Where did tiger go?" Have him find it and try to say the animal's name. Show him the dog and say, "Dog. The dog says, "Woof-woof." Line up a few animals and have him point to the different animals.

Develops/Improves: Language, vocabulary, articulation, and auditory memory skills.

17. Farm Play:

Using a play farm kit, let him have imaginative play using the animals, a barn, and other things you would find on a farm. Teach him to say the names of the animals and their sounds.

Develops/Improves: Language, vocabulary, articulation, auditory memory, creativity, and imagination skills.

18. Circus Play:

Using a play circus kit, let him have imaginative play using the animals, tent, and other apparatus you would find at a circus.

Develops/Improves: Language, vocabulary, articulation, creativity, and imagination skills.

19. Puppets:

Use puppets representing things from everyday life, such as animals, family, and career puppets, e.g., nurse, doctor, policeman, or construction worker. Place puppets on their hands and act out events.

Develops/Improves: Language, storytelling, role-playing, imagination, and socialization skills.

B. Sensory Skills: (1-20)

Sensory experiences include touch, movement, body awareness, sight, sound, and the pull of gravity. The process of organizing and interpreting this information is called sensory integration. Sensory integration provides a crucial foundation for later, more complex learning and behavior.

1. Play dough:

Use a play dough kit that includes styling tools, such as shape cutters, rolling pin, EZ squeeze dough machine, stencils, and scissors. Have him roll, squeeze, push, pull, poke, and cut play dough. Use a variety of shape cutters to cut out shapes, numbers, letters, and animals. Press small objects such as rocks, shells, and coins into the play dough.

Develops/Improves: Fine motor skills, dexterity and hand strength, eye-hand coordination, tactile tolerance, and sensory awareness through proprioceptive input.

2. Arts and Crafts:

Use foamies kits of shapes, letters, flowers, fish, animals, dinosaurs, and sports balls to stick or glue onto paper to make collages. Pour a small amount of glue on a plate to be used for gluing feathers and colored pom-poms onto paper to make collages and decorations. You can draw big circles, squares, other shapes, or animal shapes and have him glue various materials in the shaped areas. Buy holiday-related crafts so he can decorate collages for all the different holidays.

Develops/Improves: Visual perception, eye-hand coordination, tactile tolerance to different textures.

3. Finger and Brush Painting:

Place a little finger paint on paper. Have him choose a couple of colors he likes and have him play with the paint to get used to the feel of the paint on his fingers. Have him scribble with the paint. Teach him how to hold a paint brush and paint his own masterpiece. Draw a road path, simple lines and curves, shapes, letters, and numbers and have him follow with his finger.

Develops/Improves: Fine motor skills, eye-hand coordination, grasping, tactile tolerance, and sensory awareness.

4. Sponge Paint:

Using animal and shapes sponges, have him dip them into paint and sponge them onto paper to make a collage. When finished, let him clean the sponges with water. Have him squeeze them and get used to the paint and water on his hands.

Develops/Improves: Sensory awareness, tactile tolerance, eye-hand coordination, and hand strength and manipulation skills.

5. Textured Play:

Gently rub feathers, pom-poms, cotton balls, sand paper, and different textured sponges on his legs, arms, hands, belly, and back. Let him get used to the different textures. This will help alleviate tactile defensiveness. Choose only one or two textures at a time so you won't over stimulate. If the child finds this difficult, have the child do it to himself first.

Develops/Improves: Body awareness, discrimination of touch, and desensitizing to tactile sensations.

6. Odorless Shaving Cream/ Odorless Hand Lotion:

Spray shaving cream or hand lotion onto a cookie sheet or table placemat. Have him press his fingers and palms into the shaving cream and play with it. Have him rub his hands in it. You can draw or write letters, numbers, or make shapes in it. Drive a small toy car through it. Put shaving cream on the side of the tub for him to play with while taking a bath. Also use soap with different textures, such as gels, foams, liquids, and hand sanitizers.

Develops/Improves: Awareness and discrimination of touch sensation, tactile tolerance, and eye-hand coordination skills.

7. Face Painting:

Using your finger, soft sponge, cotton ball, or thin paint brush, gently paint a picture of his choice on his hand. Once he feels comfortable with this sensation, let him look into a mirror while you paint a picture on his face. This encourages him to tolerate more sensations on his face. Begin on his cheek, and then try the chin and forehead. Increase the area on his face slowly and only do as much as he can tolerate. Once he gets used to the sensation you may eventually be able to paint his whole face.

Develops/Improves: Sensory awareness and tolerance of touch sensation.

8. Deep Body Pressure Massage/Joint Compression:

Perform deep pressure and joint compression massages on arms, hands, fingers, legs, feet, toes, and back.

Develops/Improves: Provides input to tactile and proprioceptive system; calms and organizes the sensory motor systems; desensitizes and regulates the senses.

9. Bubbles:

Blow lots of bubbles all around him and then towards him. Let him try to step on and pop the bubbles. If he is afraid, just blow a few away from him and let him observe that they won't hurt him. Have him touch and clap the bubbles. Have him try to blow the bubbles.

Develops/Improves: Awareness and tolerance of sensory sensations, oral motor skills, and body awareness.

10. Echo Mike:

Let him hold an echo mike up to his mouth. Make sure he places it so it surrounds his whole mouth. Let him blow into it. Have him make sounds, say words, sing, and hum into the mike. Use other instruments like the flute and harmonica.

Develops/Improves: Oral motor skills; alleviates oral defensiveness and auditory processing difficulties.

11. Party Blowers, Pinwheels, and Whistles:

Have him blow on a party blower, pinwheel, and whistle.

Develops/Improves: Oral motor skills; alleviates oral defensiveness.

12. Feathers and Cotton balls:

Have him blow feathers and cotton balls from the palm of your hand. Then place one in his hand and have him blow it.

Develops/Improves: Oral motor skills; alleviates oral defensiveness.

13. Stamps:

Use a stamp pad and a variety of stamps to stamp pictures on paper. Use stamps of animals, shapes, flowers, dinosaurs, letters, cars, and trucks. Have him sort, pattern, and count the stamps. Place his finger on the stamp pad and have him stamp his finger print onto the paper. Put stamps on his arms and hands.

Develops/Improves: Visual-motor discrimination, eye-hand coordination, counting, and awareness of and tolerance to tactile sensation.

14. Sticker Fun:

Place a variety of stickers on paper. Use stickers of hearts, sports, balloons, animals, planets, boats, cars, holiday themes, instruments, nature, and super heroes. Put a sticker on his hand or arm.

Develops/Improves: Eye-hand coordination, counting, and awareness of and tolerance to sensory stimuli.

15. Holiday Foamies:

Use foamies decorations during the different holidays. Use glue-on foamies to make Christmas trees, Christmas stockings, gingerbread houses, flags, hearts, Easter bunnies and eggs, Halloween masks and costumes, haunted houses, and Thanksgiving turkeys. Make holiday cards.

Develops/Improves: Fine motor, eye-hand coordination, manual dexterity, and language.

16. Candid Camera:

Use a play camera with a flash to take his picture. If he hides his face, reassure him that the camera is fun. Let him hold the camera up to his eye and press down on the button to take your picture. Let him see how easy and fun it is. Smile for the camera.

Develops/Improves: Awareness and discrimination of visual and touch sensations, fine motor skills, and socialization.

17. View Finder:

Use a viewfinder with pictures of things he likes in it. Hold it up to his eyes and let it touch his face. While he looks through it, press down on the handle so the pictures change and he can view different pictures. Once he feels comfortable, let him press down and change the pictures himself.

Develops/Improves: Sensory awareness, visual discrimination, and fine motor skills.

18. Play Food:

Play with pretend food. There are great visual representations of real food. Tell your child what each food item is. Have him try and say the name of the food. Have him hold a spoon and fork. Put food in pretend pots and put lids on pots. Hold the spoon and fork and place the food on plates and pretend to eat it. Store the food in containers.

Develops/Improves: Socialization, language, creativity, and fine motor skills.

19. Play Picnic:

Using play food and utensils, tell him that you're going on a pretend picnic. Put a towel or blanket down on the floor and have him sit and play with the food. Name each food item. Have him try and say the food. Say things like, "Yummy apple!" "Do you like cookies?" Have him nod his head or say "Yes." Do this with all the foods. He can put the play food in his mouth and pretend to eat. This way you can teach him the names of different foods. Have stuffed animals and/or dolls eat with him.

Develops/Improves: Language, vocabulary, eye-hand coordination, and socialization.

20. Sand Play:

Use a sand box or sand and water table. Use a bucket to make sand castles and towers. Play with shells, cars, trucks, shovels, and other fun toys in the sand area. Great for sensory play.

Develops/Improves: Sensory awareness and discrimination of touch sensation, touch tolerance to decrease tactile defensiveness, and eye-hand coordination skills.

C. Fine Motor Skills: (1-17)

Fine motor control is the specific use of small muscles in the fingers, hands, toes, mouth, tongue, and lips. Fine motor skills include hand use, grasping, eye-hand coordination, and manual dexterity. Development of fine motor skills is necessary for activities like writing, drawing, cutting, eating, and talking.

1. Tongs and Pom-Poms:

Using kitchen tongs, have him pick up cotton balls and place them onto a plate. Teach him how to open and close the tongs with his thumb and pointer fingers. After he can pick up cotton balls, have him pick up pom-poms. This helps prepare him for using scissors. You can teach sorting here. Sort the cotton balls from the pom-poms or sort pom-poms according to color.

Develops/Improves: Color discrimination, eye-hand co-ordination, manual dexterity, and strengthens muscles of the hand.

2. Scissor Skills:

Using small plastic children's scissors (#4), have him cut along a straight line or simple curve. If he has trouble with scissors, continue practicing with the tongs and pom-poms.

Develops/Improves: Eye-hand coordination and strengthens hand muscles.

3. Costumes/Dress Up:

Using a variety of costumes that have head and face components, have him put different hats on his head and masks over his face. Use a baseball cap, cowboy hat, surgeon's cap, fireman's helmet, builder's hardhat and goggles, super-hero masks, and play sunglasses. If he resists, just hold it over his head and lightly touch his head. Do this over and over until he allows you to put it on his head. Use the same technique to get him to put things on his face. First model putting on the clothes, then have him dress up in front of the mirror.

Develops/Improves: Creativity, imagination, dexterity, body awareness, and motor planning skills.

4. Stack and Sort Board:

Sort and stack by colors, numbers, and shapes.

Develops/Improves: Eye-hand coordination, visual perception and color, number and shape discrimination, and recognition skills.

5. Instruments:

You'll need a set of toy instruments: guitar, keyboard, drum, cymbals, xylophone, shakers, harmonica, tambourine, and flute. Tell him the names of all the instruments and demonstrate how to use them. Have him play them for fun. Instruments like the guitar and keyboard have colorful, easy-to-press buttons with lights, sounds, and pre-recorded songs. Have him play and sing. Play classical or children's songs on a CD and have him play instruments to the music. March, stomp around, and dance to the music.

Develops/Improves: Oral motor, gross motor and fine motor skills, auditory discrimination, language, and memory.

6. Building Blocks:

Use a variety of blocks, such as wooden, cardboard, jumbo, and pop-up blocks. Pop-up blocks fit together firmly and are great for pushing together and pulling apart. Use jumbo cardboard boxes for stacking and crashing down. They are great for imaginative play and creative thinking skills. Build houses, castles, towers, stores, and schools. Construction is another aspect of developmental praxis and allows us to put objects together in new and different ways.

Develops/Improves: Fine motor skills, eye-hand coordination, imagination, and creativity.

7. Wooden Beads:

Have him string large, different-shaped wooden beads on a thick string. Have him pattern the beads by color and shapes.

Develops/Improves: Fine motor skills, eye-hand coordination, grasping, color and shape discrimination, and pattern sequencing skills.

8. Snap-Beads:

Push snap-beads together and pull apart. Have him pattern snap beads by color.

Develops/Improves: Eye-hand coordination, grasping, hand strength, sensory motor skills, color recognition, and discrimination skills.

9. Lace Pictures:

Have him lace string around different pictures. Have him put string in the hole and pull it up the other side.

Develops/Improves: Eye-hand coordination, grasping, and visual perception.

10. Peg Play:

Have him stack, count, sort, and pattern pegs on the textured activity mat.

Develops/Improves: Fine motor skills, eye-hand coordination, visual perception, and cognitive skills.

11. Snapping/Buttoning/Zipping Board Puzzle:

Use a puzzle with snaps, buttons, and zippers. Teach him how to snap, button, and zip clothing articles on a puzzle.

Develops/Improves: Fine motor skills, dexterity, and sensory motor awareness.

12. Work Bench:

Have him build with his own toy workbench. Have him name and use a variety of tools, such as hammer, screwdriver, screws, saw, drill, nuts, bolts, and ruler. Use tools to build houses with blocks. It is great for fine motor development to drill, screw, and unscrew nuts and bolts, and it helps develop a pincer grip.

Develops/Improves: Fine motor skills, eye-hand coordination, grasping, manual dexterity, sensory motor skills, language, and imaginative play.

13. Coloring/ Drawing:

Get simple-shape and simple-object coloring books. Have him color and scribble using various colored crayons on a blank sheet of paper. Tell him the colors of the crayons and encourage him to say them. Always encourage pronunciation of the initial consonant sounds, such as "b" for blue. Have him color in coloring books of things he likes. Color animals, shapes, holiday pictures, flowers, and trees. From ages one to two, a child holds (large) crayons with a fisted grasp. At three years of age, begin teaching the three-finger grasp. Also at age three, draw a vertical, horizontal, or squiggly line, circle, square, or triangle and have him copy it. Ask him to draw a specific shape.

Develops/Improves: Improves pre-writing skills, eye-hand coordination, grasping, and visual motor skills.

14. Popsicle Stick Play:

Make different shapes using Popsicle sticks. Have him copy the shapes you make. Make a square, rectangle, cross, triangle, star, or house, using parallel, horizontal, and vertical lines. Ask him to name the shapes. Once he learns how to make these, have him do it on his own.

Develops/Improves: Visual motor skills, eye-hand coordination, thinking, and imitation skills.

15. Puzzles:

Use a variety of floor and table puzzles to teach about the different places, objects, and things he needs to know that apply to his world. Include puzzles of types of animals (pets, farm, wild, zoo, and ocean animals), shapes, parks, transportation, instruments, food, nature, rainforests, tools, and the human body. Encourage him to say and point to different puzzle pieces; then have him place them in the correct spot.

Develops/Improves: Visual perception, spatial relationships, eye-hand coordination, and language.

16. Stacking Blocks and Cups:

Stack large blocks on top of each other. Then have him stack small blocks. Stack cups from largest to smallest and vice versa.

Develops/Improves: Eye-hand coordination, and size discrimination and sequencing skills.

17. Easel:

Let him color and scribble while standing at an easel. Draw a circle, square, and triangle, and vertical, horizontal, and squiggly lines, and have him copy them. Ask him to draw a specific shape.

Develops/Improves: Strengthens postural control and visual motor skills needed for writing activities.

D. Gross Motor Skills: (1-19)

Gross motor skills involve large muscle movement in the arms, legs, and trunk for developing and enhancing the motor coordination necessary for walking, running, jumping, and climbing. Gross motor activities stimulate and encourage development of the vestibular and proprioceptive systems, motor planning skills, body awareness, visual spatial skills, and bilateral coordination.

1. Obstacle Course:

The obstacle course should be designed to practice many kinds of movements, such as crawling, jumping, and balancing. Pick and choose what things you want in your obstacle course. 1) Crawl under a tunnel. 2) Walk across a floor balance beam (2x4 or 2x6 board). 3) Do a forward somersault. 4) Scoot under a small table. 5) Place a hula-hoop on the floor and jump in and out of the hoop. 6) Roll across a small floor mat. 7) Climb over a stack of three couch pillows. 8) Pick up a small ball and make a basket into basketball net (2-3 feet high net). 9) Roll a ball into a set of bowling pins.

Develops/Improves: Gross motor skills, body awareness, balance, spatial relationships, and problem solving. Integrates tactile, vestibular, proprioception, and visual sensations.

2. Park Therapy and Playground Play:

Have him swing, slide, go under a tunnel, climb up a fake rock-climb, hang from a monkey bar, and use the jump off apparatus. Model all the activities first. If he sees that you have fun doing them and that there is nothing to be afraid of, then he will follow through. Hold his hand during all activities until he feels safe. Once he feels safe, then he will be able to do it.

Develops/Improves: Sensory motor skills, vestibular and proprioception systems, gross motor skills, endurance, and strengthening of large muscle groups.

3. Mini-Trampoline:

Have him jump on the trampoline. Bounce around and sing different songs or listen to music.

Develops/Improves: Gross motor skills, balance, coordination, vestibular and proprioception systems, gravitational security, and language.

4. Ball Play (Age: 15 months and up; 15 minutes):

Sit on the floor with the child in front of you and roll the ball to him and have him roll the ball back to you. Tell him to say "roll" and "ball." Both of you stand up and gently toss a small ball and try to have him catch it. Then show him how to toss it back to you. Tell him to say "throw ball" and "catch ball." Begin with the underhand throw. Later try the overhand throw.

Develops/Improves: Eye-hand coordination, bilateral co-ordination, visual tracking, following directions, and attention to task.

5. Tunnel Fun:

Have him crawl through a play tunnel or tunnel tent. He can bring his favorite animals or toy to play with inside. You can crawl in with him and sing songs or play. Have a pretend picnic in the tent area. Tunnel play can be done at home or at the park.

Develops/Improves: Gross motor skills, coordination, body awareness, and spatial relations. Also provides joint compression and weight bearing on shoulder girdle.

6. Tummy Time:

Place a pillow under his belly so he is lying up on an incline. Have him do a variety of skills from this position. This position makes him use his arms more and increases weight bearing on the shoulder girdle (chest area). Stack up two or three couch pillows and have him crawl over them.

Develops/Improves: Body awareness, strengthening of shoulder girdle, gravitational security, and self-calming.

7. Copy Me:

Teach all the different body parts. Stand in front of him, touch a part of your body, and tell him to copy you. Point to different parts of your body and rhythmically say, "touch your head, nose, mouth, toes, cheeks, belly, leg, roll your hands, raise your arms, turn around, clap your hands, jump up and down, march in place, wave your hands, touch your cheeks, stick out your tongue, wriggle fingers, shake head back and forth and up and down, and make silly sounds." Then tell him to say and point to the body parts and you copy him.

Develops/Improves: Body awareness, motor planning, auditory discrimination, language skills, and eye-hand coordination.

8. Kickball:

Roll the ball and have him kick it to you. Have him run and kick a ball.

Develops/Improves: Gross motor skills, balance and bilateral coordination skills. Strengthens large muscles

9. Hoop It Up:

Use a small youth basketball and basketball hoop and have him place the ball into the hoop to make a basket. Have him pick it back up and shoot it again.

Develops/Improves: Strengthening of shoulder girdle, eye-hand coordination, visual-spatial skills, gross motor coordination, and motor planning skills.

10. Bowling:

Roll ball into pins to knock them over. Have him set them back up again. Great for learning how to take turns and compete.

Develops/Improves: Gross motor coordination, visual-spatial awareness, eye-hand coordination, motor planning, and socialization.

11. Hula Hoops:

Place three or four hula-hoops on the floor and have him jump in and out of a hoop. Then have him hop from hoop to hoop. Go in one direction, then the other.

Develops/Improves: Gross motor skills, jumping, body awareness, coordination, and balance.

12. Therapy Ball:

Using a large therapy ball, hold him and bounce him up and down on the ball. Lay him on the floor and, with consistent firm pressure, roll and press the ball up and down all over his body; this helps calm the over-stimulated child.

Develops/Improves: Body awareness, trunk control and strength, and sensory regulation.

13. Beanbag Throw:

Throw beanbags into a laundry basket. As his aim gets better, move farther back and throw them again. Teach him how to throw underhand and then throw overhand.

Develops/Improves: Eye-hand coordination and body awareness. Strengthens trunk and shoulder girdle.

14. Ring Toss:

Teach him how to toss the rings onto the sticks. As his aim gets better, move farther back and throw them again.

Develops/Improves: Eye-hand coordination and body awareness. Strengthens trunk and shoulder girdle

15. Flashlight Fun:

Shine a flashlight on different objects and toys. Hide the light and show it again. Shine the flashlight on different parts of his body and have him say what body part it is. Let your child hold his own flashlight with both hands and shine it on the wall, ceiling, and floor. Quickly move the light from spot to spot to see if he can follow.

Then slowly move the light across a wall, keeping his head still and only allowing him to follow it with his eyes.

Develops/Improves: Tracking and visual motor skills.

16. The Little Gym:

Enroll in your community's toddler, preschool, or kindergarten athletic programs to help develop strength, balance, flexibility, and gross motor coordination. Learn basic gymnastic, tumbling, and sports skills.

Develops/Improves: Gross motor skills, coordination, motor planning, balance, body awareness, and socialization.

17. Swim Lessons:

Enroll in swim lessons in your community so he can learn how to swim.

Develop/Improves: Gross motor skills, bilateral motor coordination, muscle strength, organization of sensory motor systems, and socialization.

18. Day Trips:

Take a day trip to the zoo, a museum, a play, a bowling alley, a nature walk, a farm, etc. Ask him questions about the different things he sees at each place.

Develops/Improves: Language and socialization skills.

19. Picnic in the Park:

Pack a picnic basket with all his favorite foods, a blanket, even a portable CD player, and have a relaxing picnic in the park. Sit under a big tree or next to some flowers and let him enjoy the outdoors with you.

Develops/Improves: Language and socialization skills.

E. Concept Skills:

At three years of age you can begin introducing your child to different concept skills for pre-k and kindergarten. Purchase preschool workbooks. Use flashcards and game cards to introduce concepts such as same and different, sequencing, opposites, big and small, rhyming, and matching. For math, teach counting, sorting, patterning, and numbers. Pre-writing includes letters and letter sounds. Also teach the seasons, days of the week, and months of the year.

Develops/Improves: Preschool academic skills, language, visual perception, concentration, and attention skills.

F. Bath Time Fun

Taking a bath is a great soothing activity before bed. Let him play with tub toys, splash, and enjoy the water. Let him blow bubbles in the tub or have bubble baths. He can use bathtub crayons and paint to draw on the side of the tub. Use bathtub alphabet letters to reinforce alphabet learning.

Develops/Improves: Sensory motor, grasping, and eye-hand coordination.

G. Bedtime Snuggles and Buggles:

Tell him it's time to "snuggle and buggle"; this is my endearing term for snuggling and cuddling on the bed. Snuggle up in bed or on a couch and read a bedtime story to him. You don't need to do any skills with this; you are only reading for his listening pleasure. You can allow him to pick the book. This is a great way for both of you to wind down and become calm, quiet, and peaceful before he goes to sleep.

Develops/Improves: Language and sensory motor organization (snuggling).

Conclusion:

Skills and Drills Homework: These skills and techniques can apply to all babies, toddlers, and children whether they are your typical child or have a developmental delay or a disorder like ADD, ADHD, Sensory Processing, or Autism. These methods provide structure for your child at home so he will learn how to sit, focus, follow directions, and learn a variety of different basic skills and play.

The skills and drill program can be applied to older children using learning materials that are appropriate for their age. The purpose of this is to get all students to sit and attend and master their age appropriate skill in a consistent and structured environment.

Early Childhood Intervention

Early Childhood Intervention (ECI) is a state- and federally-funded government program that provides services for babies and toddlers from birth to three years of age with disabilities or developmental delays. ECI is available in all 50 states; you can locate the ECI office in your city to establish services. In order to obtain their services, it is preferable to have a referral from a pediatrician or hospital, but you can call yourself. Your child does not have to have a diagnosis to receive ECI services. You should contact ECI as soon as you are concerned about your child's development.

After the referral, an ECI service coordinator, occupational therapist, physical therapist, or speech therapist will come to your home to complete an evaluation of your child. A service coordinator (Early Intervention Specialist) works with your family to coordinate all the services necessary to support your child's total development. The Occupational Therapist works with children to become as independent as possible in meaningful life activities as dressing, feeding, toilet training, grooming, social skills, basic play activities, fine motor and visual skills that assist in writing and scissor use, sensory integration skills, function gross motor skills and visual perceptual skills needed for reading and writing. The speech therapist helps children learn how to talk; they work on oral motor skills, expressive and receptive language, communication, and articulation. The physical therapist helps children with gross-motor body movement, balance, coordination, and strength.

These are highly qualified, trained professionals who will be able to determine if your child qualifies for services; then they will discuss with you what services will be needed. Once your child is determined eligible, you will participate as part of the ECI team in writing up an Individualized Family Service Plan (IFSP). The IFSP describes what services the child will receive, how often, and the cost of services, if applicable.

Unlike most therapies, ECI is very affordable for families and can be just as beneficial as paying for expensive private therapies. You might be assigned a monthly cost share amount determined by your health care coverage and the number of people in your family. Services are never refused if families can't afford to pay for them. Difficulties are determined on a case-by-case basis.

ECI is successful because it begins at such an early age; the earlier the intervention is provided, the better the chance that the child can improve or recover.

New Pediatric Guidelines

The good news is that in October of 2007, the American Academy of Pediatrics (AAP) made a very significant step towards early diagnosis by requiring *all* babies to be screened twice for autism by the age of two. They will require universal screenings at 18 months and 24 months, and also have some developmental screening available as early as nine months. All pediatricians will now have to become educated in autistic and sensory disorders, thus making it more likely that many babies and toddlers will be diagnosed by the age of two. The earlier the baby is diagnosed, the more effective the treatment, allowing them a greater chance for recovery. This is so critical because many children are not diagnosed until or after age five and I believe that this may be why there is not more recovery.

Notes

1. Maryann Colby Trott, M.A, Marci K. Laurel, M.A., CCC-SLP, and Susan L. Windeck, M.S., OTR/L. *SenseAbilities: Understanding Sensory Integration.* (USA: The Psychological Corporation, 1993), p. 1.
2. Trott, *SenseAbilities*, p. 1.
3. Partners in GAOLS: Marianne Aquaro, et al. *OT GOALS: Occupational Goals and Objectives Associated with Learning.* (Tucson, AZ: Communication Skill Builders/Therapy Skill Builders, 1992), p. 21.
4. www.merriam-webster.com/dictionary/medical.
5. www.merriam-webster.com/dictionary/medical.
6. www.merriam-webster.com/dictionary/medical.
7. www.merriam-webster.com/dictionary/medical.
8. www.merriam-webster.com/dictionary/medical.
9. Trott, *SenseAbilities*, p. 3.
10. Trott, *SenseAbilities*, p. 3.
11. "Kid's Are Our Business," Sante Rehabilitation Group pamphlet. (Texas).
12. Case-Smith, Jane. *Occupational Therapy for Children, 5th Edition.* (St. Louis, MO: Mosby, 2005), pp. 378-379.
13. Case-Smith, *Occupational Therapy for Children*, pp. 378-379.
14. Trott, *SenseAbilities*, p. 3.
15. Trott, *SenseAbilities*, p. 6.
16. Trott, *SenseAbilities*, p. 29

Elizabeth Burton Scott, M.A.

About the Author

Elizabeth Burton Scott is a graduate of Northwestern University in Evanston, Illinois. She has a Master's Degree in Elementary Education and is a former elementary school teacher.

She currently works as an athletic counselor and educational and Bible study teacher at the Ron Burton Training Village, a non-profit, summer sports camp for underprivileged inner-city youth located in Hubbardston, Massachusetts.

Elizabeth resides in Dallas, Texas, with her husband and son. Her mission now is to serve as a coach, consultant, and speaker for professionals and families helping children with autism. Visit www.autismprayer.com and download the full prayer for free. (Part of the prayer is on page 8.)

Robert D. Reed Publishers Order Form

Call in your order for fast service and quantity discounts!
(541) 347- 9882

OR order on-line at **www.rdrpublishers.com** *using PayPal.*
OR order by FAX at **(541) 347-9883** *OR by mail:*
Make a copy of this form; enclose payment information:
Robert D. Reed Publishers
1380 Face Rock Drive, Bandon, OR 97411

Send indicated books to:

Name_____

Address_____

City_____ State _____ Zip _____

Phone: _____ Fax _____ Cell_____

E-Mail _____

Payment by check /_/ or credit card /_/ *(All major credit cards are accepted.)*

Name on card _____

Card Number _____

Exp. Date _____ Last 3-Digit number on back of card _____

		Quantity	*Total Amount*
Raindrops on Roman by Elizabeth Scott	$14.95	_____	_____
Special Foods for Special Kids: Practical Solutions & Great Recipes for Children with Food Allergies by Todd Adelman and Jodi Behrend	$16.95	_____	_____
California Squisine: Healthy Food That's Fast, Fun and For Kids by Malcolm Kushner	$11.95	_____	_____
The Legend of Baeoh: How Baeoh Got His Stripes by Lucas Taekwon Lee	$17.95	_____	_____
101 Ways to Be a Long-Distance Super-Dad... or Mom, Too! by George Newman	$9.95	_____	_____
The Biggest and Brightest Light: A True Story of the Heart by Marilyn B. Perlyn	$16.95	_____	_____
A.D.D. The 20-Hour Solution by Mark Steinberg, Ph.D ...	$14.95	_____	_____
A Kid's Herb Book: For Children of All Ages by Lesley Tierra	$19.95	_____	_____

Quantity of books ordered: _____ Total amount for books: _____

Shipping is $3.50 1st book + $1 for each additional book: Plus postage: _____

FINAL TOTAL: _____